PUBLISHING & MARKETING
REALITIES
FOR THE EMERGING AUTHOR

A GUIDE TO HELP AUTHORS EFFECTIVELY CHOOSE
A PUBLISHING PATH & PLAN MARKETING STRATEGIES

SECOND EDITION

Publishing & Marketing
REALITIES
for the Emerging Author

A Guide to Help Authors Effectively Choose
a Publishing Path & Plan Marketing Strategies

Second Edition

by CHRISTINE ROSE

BLUE
MOOSE
PRESS

Blue Moose Press ~ Ukiah, CA
pen. produce. publish.
thebluemoosepress.com

Edited by T. S. Tate

ISBN-13: 978-1-936960-96-5
Second Edition.

ATTENTION ORGANIZATIONS AND SCHOOLS:
Quantity discounts are available on bulk purchases of this book for educational purposes or fund raising.

For more information, go to
   bluemoosepress.wordpress.com
   christinerose.wordpress.com

Library of Congress Control Number: 2013905454
Rose, Christine, 1969 -
   Publishing & Marketing Realities for the Emerging Author / by Christine Rose
1. Authorship–Publishing and Marketing. I. Rose, Christine II. Title.
ISBN-13: 978-1-936960-96-5

Printed in the United States of America

For Emerging Authors Everywhere
Do your homework
Please

TABLE OF CONTENTS

PART II: MARKETING

APPENDIX

Author's Note for Second Edition

Wow. Two years. It's been an unbelievable two years since I wrote and released the first edition of *Publishing & Marketing Realities for the Emerging Author*. Unbelievable because of what has happened in my life, personally, and unbelievable because of what has happened in the publishing industry. So very much has changed on both fronts that this book, although just a second edition, has so much new and updated information within its pages, that it could be considered an entirely new book.

For example, I no longer recommend Lightning Source, Inc. (LSI) as my first choice when self publishing. Create Space, (CS) via Amazon.com, has become my first choice for that, and this book outlines why. This isn't because LSI changed; it's because the market did. The industry changed. In fact the biggest changes for this second edition in the PUBLISHING section of the book all revolve around LSI and CS.

The way authors market books has changed somewhat as well. Things that worked moderately two years ago just does not work now. There are new options for social networking that didn't even exist two years ago. While I've kept much of the original network marketing information in this book, updating where necessary, I've expanded the marketing section with these new options as well. The Facebook section, Podcast sections, and Goodreads section are much more indepth now.

Also, I've greatly expanded the short stories section, as getting short fiction "out there" is a great way to both hone your craft and get the exposure you and your work deserve.

Read on to learn how to manage your publishing and marketing path. What worked or didn't work for me might be the opposite for you.

One thing remains, you must start building your author brand NOW, not after you're published. Or, if you're already published, then NOW NOW NOW (like yesterday, now). This means frequent content via blogging and social networking. Fresh fiction, often. Interacting with fans and readers as they grow. Being seen, both online and off.

The marketing section will show you how to do that and do it NOW.

Have I mentioned?

NOW!

Peace to you all.

Introduction: An Open Letter to the Emerging Author

Approximately 950 books are published *every single day* in the USA. That's over 345,000 books a year (Bowker)[1]. Since 2006, self-published books have increased 287%[2]. The average book sells fewer than **500 copies** *in its lifetime*[3]. This average includes books that sell millions like *Harry Potter* or *Twilight*, so there are **many** books out there selling fewer than fifty copies. According to Book Expo America (BEA), 93% of novels sell less than 1,000 copies[4].

Decide now that yours won't be one of those.

Since mid-2008, my husband and I have been touring the country, promoting our books at bookstores, festivals, and conventions. At every event, I inevitably get asked the same question: "How did you go about getting published?" or some similar variation. However, in the middle of an event, I cannot really go into a lengthy discussion of the many avenues to publish one's book, nor can I delve into the details of our complicated publishing history. It seems that people want some nice, concise answer—some sort of formula they can follow—but there is no simple formula. What works for one writer might not work for the next.

---

1 Bowker. "Publishing Market Shows Steady Title Growth in 2011 Fueled Largely by Self-Publishing Sector." Bowker. 5 June 2012. Web. 21 March 2013.
2 Bowker. "Self-Publishing Sees Triple-Digit Growth in Just Five Years, Says Bowker." Bowker. 24 October 2012. Web. 21 March 2013.
3 Anderson, Chris. "Why publishers should focus on the misses instead of the hits." *Publishers Weekly.* 17 Jul 2006. Web. 07 Apr. 2011.
4 Deahl, Rachel. "BookExpo America 2010: The Changing DIY Ethos." Publishers Weekly. 24 May 2010. Web. 07 Apr. 2011.

It depends on the writer's goals, their work, and the time they wish to devote to marketing and sales.

One day in Starbucks, because I just have to have my decaf nonfat no-whip mocha, the Barista asked what I did for a living. As I proceeded to tell her about our book and tour, she politely smiled, but her eyes glazed over in a matter of seconds. I wrapped it up quickly, not wanting to bore the poor woman. I recognized that she was just making conversation and not asking about my personal life history. After all, this has become my life. Day and night. When I get going, it can be rather hard for me to stop.

However, as I went back to my comfy chair in the corner, a patron stopped me.

"Excuse me," she said, "But I couldn't help but overhear that you're an author. How did you go about getting published?"

That's when the proverbial light bulb went on inside my dark, twisted mind. Emerging authors want to know because they want to do the same thing. This is their dream, too. They want to hear the long, convoluted story. They want to be a successful author, and they see me as a successful author, if for no other reason than I'm a living, breathing, working, published author who has sold over 5,000 books. They want to know my secret.

Of course, one can't give a complete assessment on how to go about getting published in a Starbucks or at a Renaissance Festival or a Fantasy Convention.

Still, emerging authors want to know, and I discovered that I wanted to show them, not only how to get published, as there are many options, but also how to avoid some of the common pitfalls.

The greatest problem is that there are so many options, especially in today's fast-paced, ever-changing, electronic marketplace. There is not a single way that will work for all writers. In fact, each writer will need to thoroughly examine his/her goals, energy level, and budget to determine which path will best serve them and their book.

The information on these pages will help you make that decision. Throughout the book, I will lay out the pros and cons of the four basic publishing paths from which a writer must choose. I will delve into the all-consuming world of marketing, giving you my best practices and worst mistakes.

I'm not going to sugarcoat anything. Rather, I'm going to give it to you straight. And I mean straight. I will not seduce you with promises of the New York Times Best Seller list (NYTBSL) or gala parties celebrating your genius as the latest Great American Novelist. Some of the information will sound quite harsh. Some of it will be very discouraging. You might find yourself questioning whether or not it is all worth it.

It is important to ask those kinds of questions.

But the information herein is not to burst your bubble. Rather, to give you a realistic snapshot of the options available to you and the benefits, or potential downfalls, of each. Everything in these pages I learned the hard way, so you don't have to.

Utilizing my experiences, both successes and failures, you can effectively and realistically prepare yourself for the very long road ahead. Let's stick with that metaphor for a moment. You're embarking on a long road trip, *one that will last for years,* maybe the rest of your life. It is essential to have a map so you don't take any major wrong turns, which will only serve to make your journey longer and all the more frustrating.

First. **The life of a working author is *literally* non-stop.**

Non-stop writing.

Non-stop editing.

Non-stop networking.

Non-stop promotion.

Non-stop work.

It becomes your life.

If you think you're going to be living in a penthouse suite surrounded by your bestsellers, then you have a better chance at winning the lottery.

Seriously.

If this is your only goal, save yourself a lot of frustration and spend a dollar every week playing your state lottery.

It certainly can and does happen, and, of course, if you don't play, you can't win; but you need to fully understand what you're up against.

Quitting your day job and becoming a full-time author takes great courage because it's very, very risky. In fact, I would not recommend quitting your day job at this point. Even if you have a great book that is packaged professionally and has decent distribution, it generally takes years of marketing, and multiple titles, to actually make enough money to support yourself from book sales alone.

The very first thing you must do is ask yourself these questions. Get a pen and paper (or answer right in the book), and give each question and answer considerable thought before you continue reading.

Your honest answers will help you decide which publishing path is best for you and your book.

What do you want to accomplish with your book?

When do you want this done?

Do you want to live solely off of writing, or do you just want to see your work in print? Or something in between?

Do you want to be a New York Times Best Seller (who doesn't?) By when?

Do you want to/can you travel extensively?

How much time do you want to put into marketing your book? What is your initial marketing budget?

Do you want to ultimately quit your day job? Why or why not?

How much money are you willing to invest in this venture? How much time each day? Each week?

What will you have to accomplish to feel like a "successful author"?

When is a big part of the equation here.

How much you want to work is also a big part of the equation.

Trust me. You will work *way, way, way less* at <u>any other job</u>, not to mention get a steady paycheck and benefits like health insurance, stock options, and a retirement plan, unless, of course, you're in business for yourself. If you own and run your own business, then you already know the meaning of work.

It can become your entire life.

There is nothing else.

That is what it means to be a working author:

It becomes your entire life.
Every waking moment.
Every single day.

As an emerging author, your four basic publishing choices are:

1. New York "Big Boy" Publisher (this includes the top seven publishing houses: Penguin, HarperCollins, Scholastic, St. Martin's, Harlequin, Simon & Schuster, Amazon, etc.)
2. An Independent Publisher (aka Indie or Micro-Publisher)
3. "Self-Publishing" (or an Independent Publishing House that you happen to own)
4. Vanity/Subsidy Publishing (many people call this "Self-Publishing," but I make a distinction between the two in the following section.)

PART I: PUBLISHING

Writing a book is very hard. I know. I've done it eight times now. Nine, counting this one. However, as hard as it is, writing your book is the easiest part of this process. Getting published is infinitely more difficult, especially if you go with the first of the four basic choices: a New York "Big Boy" Publisher.

1. NEW YORK BIG BOYS (NYBB)

Scholastic. HarperCollins. Penguin. Houghton Mifflin Harcourt. Simon & Schuster. Macmillan (including Tor and St. Martins). Harlequin. Little Brown, Orbit, and other imprints of the Hachette Book Group also belong in this non-comprehensive list. Believe it or now, Amazon's imprints now belong on this list as well. That's right.

These NYBB also have countless numbers of imprints that look "Indie" at first sight, but are actually a Big Boy. Do your research. And there is extensive research throughout the publishing and marketing process, so get used to doing research.

If you don't know your way around the internet, learn.

Seriously.

Remember those questions I had you answer in the introduction? You're going to start to need your answers here:

If you want your book to rocket to the top of the New York Times Best Seller list (NYTBSL), a NYBB is your best shot, and even with a

NYBB behind you, it's still a long shot. It happens every day, of course, but the ratio of authors on the NYTBSL to all authors published by NYBB is very low. Additionally, contrary to popular belief, being on the NYTBSL does not make a career. Sometimes it doesn't even make the author much money. And if it does help you earn out your advance, it is unlikely to provide residual income.

Google this: "Realities of a Best Seller Royalty Statement" and see what some best-selling authors have to say about it.

If you want a hefty five or six figure advance, a NYBB is your best shot. That said, such large advances have become the exception rather than the norm. With the recent changes seen in the industry since 2009, fewer and fewer new authors are being signed. Publishers aren't taking the risks they once were, and that means sticking with known authors who bring in the bucks. This is bad news for the new author and the little guy. Even if you are one of the fortunate ones taken under the large wing of a NYBB, advances are more in the $10,000 range, often for two books, paid out in installments over a year or longer.

This does not a living make.

If you want your book out within the next three-five years or you want more than 2-7% of the net (cover price minus printing & other costs), then you don't want a NY Big Boy.

NYBB publishing houses are working off of a century-old business model, and it's starting to affect them and their bottom line. In 2010, Dorchester Publishing went bankrupt. Others will no doubt be merging and/or following Dorchester soon. Publishers are struggling to balance their bottom lines, and part of this reason is their stance on eBooks and eBook over-pricing. More information is provided in the eBook section.

Now with Barnes & Noble damanding more money[1] for shelf space and cutting out publishers who can't (or won't) afford to give it, NYBB's authors are losing out even more.

---

1 "B&N, S&S Term Dispute Continues." *Publishers Weekly*. 25 March 2013. Web. 30 March 2013.

> ## REALITY CHECK
> Let's say, just for kicks, that you query some agents and by some miracle you get an agent to represent you this week. Another miracle, that agent gets you a publisher next week. Both are highly unlikely, by the way. However, even if these two miracles happen for you, it will still be 18-24 months before you see your book in print. If nothing else, Big Boy publishing is a long, long, long, long, slow, steep uphill road.

That's how the Big Boys work.

Now think about a more likely scenario:

You spend the next six months researching the ins and outs of every agent, which you absolutely must do. You find your dream agent and zero in on him/her, learning everything you can about them.

- Find out what they like and what they don't like.
- Read their entire blog.
- Follow them on Twitter.
- Interact with their other clients.
- Review their clients' books.
- Research queries, learning what to do and what not to do.

Then you work on your query until it's perfect, and you send it off to your dream agent. Most agents have a response time that spans from a few weeks to six months or more, and many do not allow simultaneous submissions, meaning you can't query more than one agent at a time.

After all of that, one year has already passed.

Let's say your research, query letter, and manuscript are so good, this first agent offers you representation. (Otherwise you have to start the process over again with another agent.) Congrats! You are represented in New York and are one step closer to getting published by a Big Boy.

But wait, you're still not that close.

Your new agent loves your book, but it needs a little more work. After going through the edits your agent requested (another two weeks to several months), s/he starts shopping it out. The agent then queries the publishers, just as you queried the agent. This process also takes time. Sometimes you'll hit the lottery and they'll snatch it up, but usually it's several months. Before you know it, another year has passed. And this is all before a publisher says YES.

From the time you started this process, two years have passed. Then you finally get that YES, and it was all worth it...but you're still not done.

After a publisher says YES and you get your contract, it's time for more rewriting, editing, and polishing. Like I said, another 18-24 months to publication from the YES. By the end of the process, two to four years have gone by for your first book. Hopefully in the meantime, you have been writing other books, so the subsequent books, if your first one sold well enough, will not take so long. Hopefully, too, your first book does well enough that your publisher will pick up the others.

Additionally, Big Boy or not, it's up to the **author** to market him/herself and their book. Unless you win the lottery a third time (that's after getting an agent and a big publisher with a fat advance), you won't get any marketing budget from the publisher. If you're really lucky, you **_might_** get matching funds for your out-of-pocket marketing expenses.

And if you thought getting a publisher was hard, it's a huge piece of dark chocolate cake next to marketing your book, the second part of the equation. During this entire two-to-four-year process, you should be building your online networks, blogging, and making connections, online and off, that will help you once your books are on the shelves... all while writing more books and short stories.

> **REALITY CHECK**
> With a Big Boy, your book has three months (90 days) to make its mark, or they go onto the next book. If it isn't selling well, your book is dropped, but the NYBB still has the rights, so you can't do anything else with it.

Congratulations! Your book is now on the shelves in every major bookstore across the nation!

That said, with a Big Boy, you will have the benefit of their in-house publicist, their impressive name, their media and industry contacts, prolific distribution, and possibly excellent bookstore placement, which is how the majority of brick-and-mortar shoppers find their next book. Visibility is what it's all about. If you aggressively market on top of this, you have a good chance of earning back your advance, which in the eyes of the Big Boys, is a fine success. They will likely buy your next book, and so on.

However, again, it's extremely difficult (read: near impossible) to get a NYBB as your publisher, especially in since the huge industry shift that started in 2009. I've said it before, but it's worth repeating: Big Boys are taking on fewer and fewer new authors every day. Money is too tight and the industry is changing too fast for them to take that risk.

It happens, of course, but the odds are akin to winning the lottery. Seriously.

This is not to discourage you. If you write well and you have a lot of patience and can invest years into the process, Big Boys are the way to go. You'll have the validity and the prestige. You'll have fabulous distribution. Once in, you'll have the best shot at becoming that best-selling author. Once in, many publishers will treat you like family.

So, based on your answers to the questions from the introduction, you have decided that New York Big Boy is the best publishing path for you.

Now here is how to get one:

First, you absolutely must go through a literary agent. NYBBs, as a rule, do not take unsolicited submissions. Although author Dean Wesley Smith claims differently in *Killing the Sacred Cows of Publishing*[1] (also linked directly from my blog[2]), and it is well worth the read. Getting a literary agent takes huge amounts of research, a query letter even more polished than your completed novel, a very high tolerance for rejection, unlimited patience, and an unwavering positive outlook.

1 Smith, Dean Wesley. *Killing the Sacred Cows of Publishing.*
(*http://www.deanwesleysmith.com/?page_id=860*)
2 http://christinerose.wordpress.com on the "References" page.

LITERARY AGENTS

Literary agents are those elusive, magical creatures who will help you and your book rocket to the NY Times Best Seller list (NYTBSL). Without agents, you have virtually no chance in getting a NYBB publisher, which is your best (but certainly not your only) chance in becoming a best-selling author on a grand scale.

Before you ever contact even ONE literary agent, there are three things you absolutely must do:

1. **Finish and polish your book.** This means have more people than just your family members read it. Have beta reading groups, writing groups, online critique or writing critique groups give you their critiques as well. (Sometimes for non-fiction, an agent will only require a book proposal, but this book focuses mostly on fiction writers.)

2. **Research**. And I mean extensive research that will likely take three to six months of your time before you ever send your first query. More on this below.

3. **Write and revise and revise and revise and revise and revise your query letter** based on the information you found in the aforementioned research. Then get it critiqued and revise it again.

I'm not kidding.

Literary agents get between 75 and 500 queries every single day. Most of them are subpar queries from writers who didn't do the above three things. These are easily deleted by literary agents, but it also puts them in a mood to hit the delete button going forward. I can't begin to imagine how exhausting it must be wading through their slush[1] pile. Query after query, several of which brag about how wonderful their novel is and how it's going to make said agent rich, day after day after mind-numbingly boring day.

While preparing to search for an agent, I participated in Nathan Bransford's *Agent for a Day*[2] exercise in 2009, and I was shocked to realize what a literary agent goes through daily.

---

1 slush pile = unsolicited manuscripts
2 http://blog.nathanbransford.com/2009/04/be-agent-for-day-here-we-go.html

On a very, *very* light day.

Read this entire exercise from beginning to end[3]. This will put you in your prospective agent's position. From this perspective you will write a better query letter.

Then I suggest you read his entire blog[4] in full, as part of your research. I'll also list other blogs for you to research in the Appendix.

If you really want that NYBB, you will need to do all these things first.

There are no shortcuts.

Don't send a query they can easily delete.[5]

Don't give them a reason to delete it.

They don't need a reason to delete it.

They need a reason *not* to delete it.

DO THE RESEARCH.

THE RESEARCH

Before you ever submit a query to an agent, you have to get to know them. *Each and every one of them[6]*.

Don't submit a Young Adult (YA) story to an agent who says they do not represent children's books, unless they specify that YA is okay. YA is a fuzzy area—some consider them children's, some don't. Know what they accept and what they don't.

Learn about who they are. Their choice in client leans heavily on those who make a personal connection with the agent in question. It has to do with what they like. What they need. What they choose to represent. What they can **sell**.

Agents don't care that "everybody" likes your book. Whether that "everybody" is friends and family or whether you've actually tested the market.

---

3 All referenced items are listed in footnotes, in the Appendix, and linked directly to the internet source from my blog http://christinerose.wordpress.com on the "Resources" page.

4 http://blog.nathanbransford.com

5 http://www.agentquery.com/writer_hq.aspx

6 LitStack has a segment where they speak to industry professionsals, a great way to get to know the agents and learn more about the future of publishing. http://litstack.com/?cat=25

Agents don't want to hear how you are going to make them a lot of money, because they hear that countless times a day. Read the *Query Shark* blog[1] in full. <u>In Full</u>. And you'll see what I'm talking about.

> ### REALITY CHECK
> Rachelle Gardner, of the WordServe Literary Agency, blogged about her slush pile for 2010. She received over 10,000 queries. How many clients did she find through those cold queries? ZERO. That's right. Not one query resulted in representation with this agent. She found new clients through conferences, referrals, and even blogging.

Seriously.[2]

Ms. Gardner has since deleted that post (how interesting!), but her client Judy Hedland's reference to it in her blog[3] still exists.

New York Publishing is changing so fast at the moment that many agents are finding other jobs. Nathan Bransford, mentioned earlier, is no longer an agent. He is now an author. Colleen Lindsay, of #queryfail fame, left the FinePrint Literary Agency to take a job in business development at Penguin.

The system is in flux.

Do your research.

When you think you've done enough,

You haven't.

Do some more.

It is changing every day.

---

1 http://queryshark.blogspot.com/ -- Dedicated to writing and critiquing query letters. A polished query is an essential first step to breaking the slush-pile barrier. Spend considerable time and energy ensuring your query is stellar before even contacting your first agent.

2 Gardner, Rachelle. "New Query Policy...and 2010 Stats." *Rants and Ramblings: On Life as a Literary Agent.* 8 Jan. 2011. Web. 30 Mar. 2011.

3 Hedlund, Jody. "Is the Query System Dying?" Jody Hedlund: Author & Speaker (blog). 10 Jan. 2011. Web. 07 Apr. 2011.

My Personal Experience with Agents

When we left our first publisher in April 2009, I briefly thought about looking for an agent. In fact, I even spoke directly with an agent, whose attention I had gained through my Twitter presence. When the fact that my marketing abilities helped sell nearly 2,000 copies of my book in the first four months didn't impress this agent, I decided against seeking representation. Here is why:

Selling 2,000 copies in four months is no small feat for a first-time author with a small indie publisher. In fact, our indie publisher couldn't financially keep up with the print demand. Remember, 2,000 copies is four times the amount the average book sells in its lifetime. The agent acknowledged that it was indeed impressive, but it wasn't enough. When I told the agent how people responded to the book, how I received countless emails about how they couldn't put it down, etc., this agent responded, "Now you have to get an editor to feel that way about it."

That's when I was done. I had thousands of readers who said they loved it, but I had to impress a single person. Not for this writer. For me at that point in our YA *Rowan of the Wood* series, it was too much work and risk to wait possibly years to get the sequel out. I didn't want our growing readership to have to wait that long, so I chose a different route.

Interestingly, nearly a year later, another agent found me via Twitter, or rather found my alter ego O. M. Grey (Twitter: @omgrey). As a marketing experiment, I created the persona O. M. Grey to author my Steampunk[4] paranormal romance book *Avalon Revisited*. The entire Olivia experiment can be found in the Marketing section of this book. So, now both Christine & Ethan Rose and O. M. Grey are proud to be represented by Louise Fury of the L. Perkins Agency.

Still. This is the exception, not the rule. I do believe, however, more and more agents will be finding clients this way. They want authors who know how to market themselves. Those are the authors that will survive the change, according to my agent.

---

4 Steampunk is a sub-genre of Science Fiction/Fantasy set in the Victorian Era, where all of the technology is powered by clockwork or steam. Thus the term Steampunk.

WHAT AGENTS WANT

- A query letter that causes them to pause and take their finger off the delete key. **Voice**. Good writing.
- Something they can **sell** <u>This is the key</u>. Because if they can't sell it, they don't get paid, then they can't pay their own mortgage, bills, etc. Remember, an agent doesn't make a dime until you do. If they're asking for payment up front, they are not a reputable agent. Get familiar with the Predators & Editors website.[1] There is a depressing amount of people out there trying to make their living from preying on emerging authors' dreams and ignorance. Don't be one of their victims.
- Something agents can sell is often something that can be put into a pre-labeled box. The NY publishing industry really likes boxes with very clear labels. I was once told that I would have to rewrite my YA series in first person for it to sell as a YA book. Nonsense. There are countless YA books out there in complete omniscient POV[2]. I've just recently read two of them. But that's the box NY had currently chosen, so that's what they were looking for.
- Agents don't like crossovers or genre mashups. Again. The box. It doesn't matter that the best-selling series of the 21st century is a YA crossover. Agents want to put anything new in a box. It's easier to pitch to the publishers because that's what the publishers want.
- Many agents don't like prologues or series. Go figure. My editor tells me this isn't true anymore. Next week, it might be again. Serioulsy, it fluctuates that quickly sometimes.

I'm not saying that this makes any sense. This is just what I've learned being out in the publishing trenches since 2007.

What I do know is this: the better you know the agent you're querying, the better chance you have at standing out amongst their enormous

1 http://pred-ed.com
2 POV = Point of View

slush pile. The better you know the agent, the better chance you have in writing a query letter that will result in a positive response.

Use something like QueryTracker[3] to help you keep track of the agents you research and ultimately query. Several agents will not allow simultaneous submissions. That means if you query them, you had better not query anyone else until you hear back from them. It's well-worth the $25/year for the premium account.

Find your top ten agents. Do even deeper research on them. Follow their blogs for a month or two before you query. Follow them on Twitter. Get to know them as people. Review the books of their other clients and post them on your blog, promote them on Twitter[4]. This strategy worked very well for a colleague. This way, your dream agent *sees you*.

Then your query has to knock their socks off.

After those rejections, do the next group. It can take up to six months for an agent to respond to your query. If you're not getting a request for a partial for every third query (and you're submitting to the right agents in the right way, due to your research), then there is something wrong with your query. Revise it again.

Did I mention this was time consuming?

This is where the publishing route could take four years or more to see your book in print. If you don't want to wait, then this isn't the avenue for you. More than anything, you must have unlimited patience when dealing with New York.

Patience while researching.

Patience during the query process.

Patience after you find an agent.

Patience after you find a publisher.

So send that query out, set yourself a follow up reminder on your phone or calendar[5] in six weeks, then forget about it. Go write your next short story or start on a new novel. Keep writing. When your reminder goes off, follow up and set a new reminder, et cetera. Then go back to

---

3 http://querytracker.net
4 If you don't have a blog or Twitter account, time to get one. More in the Marketing section.
5 iCal or other calendars aer great for setting yourself reminders for such things, as well as keeping track on how much time you're spending marketing and writing. Let technology help keep your mind free to write.

writing. It is essential to keep writing and to continue sending your work out. Then, once it tips for you, you will have a pile of manuscripts ready to go.

Truly, there are so many DOs and DON'Ts for agents, I can't put them all here, and it would only be repeating what's elsewhere anyway. This is the part where you have to do your research.

Get well acquainted with Google.

TIPS:
- Don't think that you're the exception. You're not.
- Don't think that they'll love your pitch so much they'll represent something they don't normally represent. They won't.
- You are not the exception. I mean it.
- In their eyes, you are another wannabe author who needs them. If you give them any reason to pass you over, they will. They don't need a reason to pass you over. They need a reason not to.

Trust me. Finding an agent will be your full-time job for three months to a year, or more. It's a commitment. It's a lot of work and research, but it will be worth it when you hold that five-or-six-figure advance in your hands from HarperCollins.

The only way to win that lottery is to play their game.

It is a huge risk, but it all depends on what you want.

PRO/CON LIST FOR THE NYBB PUBLISHING PATH

PROS

- Huge publishing name behind you
- Possible marketing budget and in-house publicist
- Industry connections
- Media connections
- Prestige
- Best shot at New York Times/USA Today Best Seller List
- Likely decent-to-good bookstore placement
- **** Extensive Distribution ****
- Possible hefty advance

CONS

- Landing an agent *and* NYBB publisher are about as likely as winning the lottery. Twice. Remember 75-500 queries every. single. day.
- You get a very, very small percentage (2-7%) with a NYBB.
- It's still up to you to market your book, and you see less return per book.
- It will take three to five-plus years to see your book in print.
- They give your book ninety days to make a splash, then they go onto the next one. There's always a next one.
- The publishing industry is in a great state of flux at the moment. Things are changing, but the NYBB aren't changing with them. They're still working off a century-old business model.
- After all of the research and querying you may still not get an agent.
- After getting an agent, you may still not get a publisher. Now you're two to three years into this process, so what's next?
- It's, as you can see from the above two, very risky. However, the reward can be great. If you have the patience and the talent, not to mention a full-time day job to support you in the mean time, definitely go this route.

2. INDEPENDENT PUBLISHER

(aka Micro Press, Indie Press)

If you've decided that it's all just too much or will take too long or is too uncertain to try for a NYBB Publisher, your next choice is a smaller, independent publisher.

Now indie publishers can range from large companies with dozens of employees to a "mom & pop" publishing company run by just one or two people. Some may have an agreement with a distributor, some may not. Some give advances, and some do not. Some actually require submissions strictly through a literary agent, so you're back to trying to find one of those.

In this day and age, nearly every indie publisher will have a website which contains their submission guidelines. Follow them. Here again is where you have to do some research and follow simple directions, just like you would have to find an agent.

If they publish solely paranormal romance, don't submit general fiction.

Common sense, really.

You'll also want to follow the same instructions for writing a query letter, as if you were writing one for a literary agent. It's still a good idea to know something about the publisher, their acquisitions editor, and what they like. They probably have blogs. The internet is an amazing resource. Use it. Not tech savvy? **Learn.**

When you leave the realm of literary agents and NYBB Publishers, you have to start watching out for total scams. There are many people out there who want to prey on your dreams.

Don't let them.

Things to watch out for: (Seriously, pay close attention to these. I have met author upon author with horror stories of indie publishing experiences. Everything from losing all their rights, even their own copyright, which should always be in the author's name, to losing tens of thousands of dollars.)

> ### *ANY PUBLISHER who asks for money up front is <u>not</u> a traditional publisher.*

They are a vanity/subsidy press trying to masquerade as traditional publishers. A traditional publisher takes on a huge part of the financial risk, that's why they get such a big cut (at least 80%, usually more).

- Traditional publishers pay for
  - the editor.
  - the proofreader.
  - the cover artist.
  - the ISBN numbers.
  - the print runs.
- They format and layout the book.
- They deal with the Library of Congress and the US Copyright office.
- They send out review copies at their expense (both printing and shipping).
- They help you set up book signings and should have a nice release party for your book. They pay for your book tour, at least in part.
- They, hopefully, have distribution, or else your book won't be available in stores.
- You will get X# of copies of your book for free, but you will have to buy other copies from them for your own purposes/events. This should most definitely be at least for 50% of the cover price.

BUT BEWARE
If a publisher says something like:
"The more books you buy from us,
the more it will help us out."
RUN!
<u>Very</u> <u>fast</u> in the opposite direction.

This indicates that they do not have the working capital to invest in a proper print run without your (the author's) financial help. Unfortunately, going with an Independent Press can be the worst choice of your writing career. You will not only lose your publishing rights, but they will overprice your book and your eBook, neither of which you have any control over, leaving you with no option but to abandon that book. I've seen it happen, more than once, to talented authors with excellent books that have been lost to obscurity.

The fact is many Independent Publishers don't have the capital to effectively publish your book and justify their hefty percentage.

Here's how it works:

- Publishers get books printed for a fraction of the cover price. Take for example a paperback book of about 240 pages, 8.5×5.5 in size. It should cost between $1.50 and $3.50 per book to print, depending on the size of the print run. The more in a print run, the less the cost per book.

- For a small print run of 1,000 books, that's $3,000 at $3.00, a high estimated figure for 1,000 books. If they're charging you 50% of the cover price (say, $7.48 for a cover price of $14.95[1], because novels are always overpriced with a small, indie press), you're paying that $3,000 for 401 books. They just got 599 books without *__any__* financial risk of their own. **For free** because you just paid for the print run.

- Yet, they're taking at least 80% of the sale price from the print run you funded.

You might as well publish it yourself, if this is the case.

However, again, if you just want to see your book in print and not worry about any of the publishing aspect, if you don't plan on doing much promotion, or if it will just be an after-work hobby for you, this type of publisher can work for you.

Just know what you're getting into.

---

1 These printing costs are an average compiled from a sampling of several POD and short-run printers. The retail prices listed are for novels (fiction), nonfiction is based on a different pricing model. For example, a 240 page nonfiction book sells easily for $15-20, but for fiction, that's seriously over-priced. Perusing Amazon.com or the shevles of any bookstore can show you the difference in pricing for the same size book between fiction and nonfiction.

Same as with the Big Boys, and every other publishing option, promoting your book is up to you. With the independent publisher, they, too, might have an in-house publicist at your disposal. That's a good thing. It also means they make enough to have employees, another good sign that they are a viable business.

> **ADVICE**
> Unless a publisher gives you an advance, even if it's a small, token advance, they're not going to have the capital or the incentive to really push your book.

Don't sign away your rights for nothing.

Be sure to check out Predators & Editors[2] before signing anything. It's certainly not comprehensive, but it's a start.

The previous pages contain a brief overview of things to watch out for with an Independent Publisher. Actually, most of those things show you how to see through a scam. "Publishers" who do those things aren't traditional publishers. (By the way, if they go out of their way to assert they're a "traditional publisher," then they're probably not.)

An *actual* Independent Publisher might be perfect for your book because you get the benefit of traditional publishing:
- Someone sharing the risk and the reward
- Distribution in all major retail outlets
- A team behind you in your journey
- The validation and prestige of being a published author, which means someone other than you believed enough in you/your book to invest in it.

---

2 http://pred-ed.com/

- You don't have the stigma of being "self-published." Granted, this stigma is lessening, but it is still there.

An independent publisher should be your partner in this journey. One of the greatest reasons to go Indie is the close relationship one can have with their publisher and editor.

Indie publishers aren't running a multi-billion dollar corporation. They're generally more about the author.

For example:

- You, as an author, might get more say in your cover art (something that almost never happens with a NYBB).

- You will likely get a higher percentage than with a NYBB. With an Independent Publisher, your percentage will be between 10%-20%, as opposed to 2%-7% with a NYBB.

- Before signing with any publisher, ask around. Ask their other authors (note: plural) what doing business with them is like. Because, bottom line, this is a business.

  - Do they pay royalties on time? If there are no royalties to pay out, do they at least send your reports on time?

  - Do they keep the author in the loop?

  - Do they assist in any marketing efforts?

  - Are they reasonable to work with or is it one drama after another?

  - Do they support the author's marketing efforts?

  - Do they send out review copies? To whom? How many? Is there a cap?

  - Have they ever fallen behind in keeping up with the demand of a book?

- Don't be so over-the-moon about someone wanting to publish your work that you don't protect yourself legally and financially. This is still <u>YOUR</u> work. Your baby. Your book. And you should benefit from it at least as much as the other "middle men;" i.e., publisher, distributor, wholesaler, etc.

Again, if they're giving you at least a few thousand dollar advance, they'll be more committed to your success than if they give you nothing.

Don't kid yourself. It's all about the money to *any* business, and the publishing business is certainly not an exception.

If they invest in your book with an advance, you better believe they're going to work very hard to get a return on that investment.

> ### ADVICE
> Don't sign with *any* publisher unless they are giving you some kind of advance.
> **Don't sign away your rights for nothing.**

Many Independent Publishers are also authors who publish their own books as well as others'. This is totally fine! Some Indie Publishers started publishing companies so they could publish their own books, but you must ensure that your book's success is more important to them than their own book's success.

As a publisher, if they have more than three different authors, they've gained a level of validity in the industry. The Library of Congress won't allow a publisher to get In-Publication-Data unless they've published at least three different authors and are "most likely to be widely acquired by U.S. libraries."[1]

Ten different authors under one publishing house gives them a higher level of validity. Ingrams, the largest book wholesaler in the US, won't even look at a publisher until they've published ten different authors. (There is a way to go through Ingrams without this, but I'll save this for the next section about "self-publishing.")

Just ensure this Independent Publisher is not using your book to validate their publishing business, so they can publish more of their own books. Talk with their other authors--several of them--and get their story/opionion on working with this publisher.

Basically, are they an author-first or a publisher-first house?

---

1 http://cip.loc.gov/

My Personal Experience with an Independent Publisher

Our original publisher, to whom I will refer as merely The Publisher Who Shall Not Be Named (PWSNBN), took us for a bumpy ride; however, after talking with other of their authors, we got off easy.

After trying for an agent for about six months (I now know that is nowhere near long enough to search) with no luck, Ethan and I decided that we would just publish our novel ourselves back in 2007. As a last ditch effort, I read an article written by a local publisher, and I sent a query. They were interested in our novel and decided to publish it. Our book was scheduled for release in eight months, very fast compared to NYBB, no doubt. I made it very clear that we were going to aggressively market our book and travel the country doing so. I started making plans for the release of our book, which was supposed to be August 2, 2008. We scheduled several events, and it wasn't until late July that we were told our official release would be pushed back until October. All those pre-paid conventions and festivals were now pointless, as we would not have a book in-hand to promote until October. These things happen, we told ourselves, as there are always delays in publishing. We did some local events in late 2008, and I went all out with costume contests and spooky treats, all under a Halloween theme. As I told the PWSNBN, we were going to be aggressive.

By early 2009, we were on the road, promoting our book as aggressively as I knew how. We ended up traveling 19,000 miles throughout 2009 in our Geekalicious Gypsy Caravan[1] promoting the book and preparing for the sequel. In the midst of blogging daily, making two video blogs (vlogs) a week for YouTube (TheTuberRose), hosting a BlogTalkRadio show once a week, and visiting between two and three bookstores a week, I also started researching agents and how to query properly. I was determined to find an agent and a new publisher for our sequel, as the PWSNBN proved to be quite difficult to work with. (Side note: no publisher will pick up a series in mid-series. Just FYI)

---

1 aka GGC, a travel trailer painted to advertise our books. Photo on page 47.

However, just after we returned home from the second leg of the tour in early April 2009, I started getting calls and emails from several Barnes & Nobles about our upcoming third (and longest) leg of our nationwide tour. This time we would be gone for five months straight, traveling from Texas up through Minnesota, the Dakotas, Utah, Colorado, over to Washington State and back across the continent to New York before settling in Kansas and finally coming back to Texas at the end of October. This entire tour had been planned and mostly paid for. These calls and emails from Barnes & Nobles all said the same thing: "We can't get your book."

Really?

I was about to embark on a two-week blog tour in which I was going to give away a $360 Kindle 2, among other contest giveaways, on top of my normal marketing efforts. I frantically called the PWSNBN and asked her why the bookstores couldn't get our books. She said that we would have to buy more books from her so she could afford another print run.

Again. Really?

At this time in our business relationship, we had already sold over 1,000 books (first five months of release) through their distributor, and Ethan and I had sold another 2,000 on the road. We were by far the best-selling book of the PWSNBN, but it became very obvious that did not matter to this publisher. If we canceled this tour because the publisher couldn't afford to print the books, we would lose thousands of dollars. At the same time, it was not our responsibility to fund the print run.

So I fought to get our rights back.

The PWSNBN had been hounding me to sign an updated contract during the early months of 2009, but I had yet to sign as it took more rights and higher percentages. It even took the rights to our characters. By this time, the PWSNBN had already been several weeks late with the accounting report and failed to pay us our royalties, so we were able to get out of our original contract on a technicality and move forward on our own, salvaging most of our summer tour. Lucky for us, as other authors under the PWSNBN did not get out so easily. They had to sign a non-disclosure agreement, which likely tells you all you need to know about their experience with the PWSNBN.

So, yes. Be very careful.

PRO/CON LIST FOR THE INDIE PUBLISHING PATH

PROS

- Validity and prestige of being picked up by a publisher
- A team working with you that is usually very author-centered
- Possible marketing budget & in-house publicist, depending on size
- Possible industry connections
- Possible media connections
- Possible[1] good distribution and stocked in bookstores
- Possible advance
- With some indie publishers, you'll be able to keep some of the publishing rights, like merchandising, movie/TV, electronic, etc... not an option at all with NYBB.
- You get a larger percentage (10-20%) than a NYBB (2-7%)[2].
- Many indie publishers are actually in a better financial state in the current economy than the NYBB are at the moment.
- You can retain more control over your book and not have to deal with the publishing end of it (ISBN #s, Library of Congress, US Copyright, printing costs, etc.)

---

1 Sorry for all these *possibles*, but it's just a wide variety. It really depends on the size publishing house, the relationships they've built in the industry, and what they offer.

2 Still, 2% of 100,000 books is a lot more than 20% of 2,000 books, plus more people are reading your book. Don't look at this for the money only. There is truly no money in publishing.

CONS

- It's still up to you to market your book, and you have to share the returns
- It will take one to three-plus years to see your book in print after acquisition
- As with any publisher, if after you sign the papers they don't treat you or your book well, you could have just lost the right to publish or find another publisher for years. Know what you're signing. Talk to <u>several</u> of their other authors. Have an escape clause in the contract if they don't hold up their end of the bargain (like paying you royalties on time, sending you accounting reports on time, and keeping the book in print; i.e., keeping up with the print demand).
- There are a gazillion indie publishers out there, and it's up to you to research which are legit, which are mostly "self-publishers," or worse, thinly veiled Vanity Publishers, and which ones are crooks.

3. "SELF-PUBLISHING"

The term "self-publishing" is quite fuzzy. The boundaries of this choice bleed into both Independent Publishers on one end and Vanity Publishing on the other, thus the quotation marks. For the purposes of this book, I'm defining "self-publishing" as a writer who publishes their own book through a publishing company they own, as opposed to publishing through a Vanity or Subsidy Press. If you're paying a POD[3] publishing service like iUniverse, Xlibris, or AuthorHouse, you are using a vanity press, and they will be covered in the next section. Basically, if the logo on the spine is your company, you are a "Self-Publisher."

Unfortunately for those authors who produce quality work, self-publishing carries a nasty stigma. Many readers, upon hearing the words "self-published," conjure up images of badly Photoshopped covers, poor layout, and shoddy writing. And for good reason. This describes many

---

3 POD = print on demand

(really, far too many) self-published books. In fact, I've seen simply atrocious book covers from an Independent Press that houses over sixty authors! On the other hand, I've seen gorgeous covers from both Indie Presses and "Self-Publishers," alike.

In short, there is no quality control in self-publishing unless the author takes it upon him/herself to ensure said quality. More often than not, this means a considerable investment in professional editors and proofreaders, graphic artists, and desktop publishers.

However, many "self-published" books are excellent. They contain fresh, new ideas that don't fit into the NYBB box. They are genre mashups. They are unique and witty and fun. They are dark and edgy. Many readers seek out self-published works because they enjoy something other than the same-ol', same-ol'. With the growing popularity of eBooks, readers can try out new authors for less of a financial risk. With the Kindle, they can try out any eBook for no financial risk. Plus, if you take my advice and keep your eBook priced reasonably, this benefits the author, who gets a larger readership, as well as the reader, who finds something fresh for just a few dollars.

As for the stigma that all "self-published" books are of low quality, I say, balderdash. Some are great. Some suck. Truly, the same can be said about books published through the Big Boys. Some are great. Some suck. But those from the NYBBs are all professionally edited, laid out, and designed.

This is what the "self-published" author must take on him/herself, and it's no small feat. We've paid professional editors to edit and proof our novels, and they still come back with too many errors. It requires several passes from more than just two or three sets of eyes. And please remember, *you cannot edit your own work*. You will not see what another set of eyes will see. You know what you're trying to say. You know what you mean. You must ensure that what you mean is actually what you wrote. This requires more eyes than just your own.

Invest in the quality of your book.

Once it's out there, it's out there for good.

There has never been a better time to "self-publish" your work. There have never been so many avenues and affordable options to get your book published, and there have never been so many outlets through which to sell your book.

I will walk you through exactly how to have a quality book that is available in bookstores and maybe even finds some shelf space of its own.

As an author, the greatest thing about owning your own publishing house is that you can do things your way. You don't have to worry about being taken advantage of by those preying on your dreams.

Your destiny is in your hands…and yours alone.

If you succeed or if you fail, it's all up to you.
Rather terrifying, isn't it? Also, quite exciting.
Your destiny is in your hands.
Take a deep breath and dive in.

The worst thing about owning your own publishing house is the amount of work and money involved. It is, by far, the most expensive way to get your book professionally and legitimately published. No doubt.

However, it also has the greatest potential for reward. And, as in everything, the higher the risk, the greater the reward.

Sure, you can sit back and write all day, every day; but not if you want your books to sell. Not until you're at the level of James Patterson or Sue Grafton or, to cite a self-published author, J. A. Konrath can you do nothing but write every day. There is marketing to do, and it is all up to you. Remember, this is true for whichever of the Four Basic Choices you choose[1].

Although, as I type these words, this model is changing. The entire industry is changing so fast; it's rather difficult to keep up. Several self-published authors are now finding that they can market less and write more thanks to Amazon's Kindle sales. More about this in the extensive eBook section.

---

1 Although that worked well for Amanda Hocking. Write nine books while looking for that NYBB. If you don't find one, publish all nine on Kindle at once. Once they're hooked, keep them hooked.

Ultimately, however, some promotion will be needed no matter what. Even those self-published authors who are selling well in eBooks and on the Kindle are at least blogging, tweeting, and participating in other social media on a daily basis.

If you want your book to sell, it's up to you to promote it.

Additionally, however, as the publisher, it is also your responsibility to get the book professionally edited, laid out, and printed. You must also take care of things like Copyright and LCCN numbers…not to mention the all-too-important ISBN number.

These things and more are now your responsibility as the publisher.

First, you must establish a company and, preferably, make it an LLC[1], as it gives you another level of legal protection. Depending on the state in which you incorporate, and if you do it yourself or hire a lawyer, this can run from hundreds of dollars to thousands.

With a publishing company comes other responsibilities that I won't go into here, as a book called *Dan Poynter's Self-Publishing Manual* covers this comprehensively. It will take you through everything in setting up your own publishing house, step-by-step. There is now also a second volume that talks you through the latest technologies.

ISBNS

After you have your business entity set up, you have to get an ISBN (International Standard Book Number) for your book. Currently, there are some who say the ISBN is dead[2]. It might be the case in the near future, but for now it is still the norm and rather essential if you want your books to be available in bookstores, in libraries, and in the iBookstore for the iPad. Please **DO NOT** buy a single ISBN number, especially from LuLu, but not even from Bowker[3]. I know it's less money in the short run, but you will not own that ISBN, another company will. Plus, you will use at least two ISBNs per title, maybe more if you go into audiobooks, hardbacks, and the like. In the long run, you will save money by buying a block of ISBNs from Bowker IdentifierServices

1 Limited Liability Corporation. Such an entity limits owner's liability.
2 Carins, Michael. "The ISBN Is Dead." *Personanondata*. 04 Aug. 2009. Web. 02 Apr. 2011.
3 Industry resource for ISBNs and other bibliographic information

(TM)[4]. Plan to buy a block of at least ten ISBNs for around $250. If you will be participating in an author co-op, explained shortly, consider pooling some money and buying 100 ISBNs for just $525. Ten or 100 may seem like a lot of ISBN numbers, but it's really not. You need a unique ISBN for every version of the book. (e.g., hardback, paperback [trade], paperback [mass market], audio book, eBook [Kindle], second editions, cover changes, etc.). They add up fast.

TIP

If you take my forthcoming advice and go with Lightning Source or CreateSpace as a distributor/printer, do not buy a UPC symbol along with your ISBNs from Bowker, because you get one for free with your book setup.

INTERIOR AND EXTERIOR PROFESSIONALISM

PAY A PROFESSIONAL EDITOR. I mean it. Don't scrimp here. This can cost from $150–$5,000 or more, depending on the editor you choose and their rates. Some editors charge by the word, and others charge by the manuscript. We had a freelance editor contact us who charges $0.06 per word. For a short 65,000 word YA novel, that's nearly $4,000, a little too rich for most small publishers. Certainly too rich for me. The most we ever paid for editing services resulted in the worst editing job I have ever seen before or since. Ask around. Get references. Look in the Appendix of this book for suggested freelance editors. They do good work for reasonable rates.

Pay a professional proofreader. This is not always the same person as the editor. $15/hr to $150/hr. Some charge per word. Ask your editor if they also provide proofreading services.

If you do not know how to layout a book in InDesign, QuarkXpress, or a similar program...

PAY SOMEONE TO DO IT

---

4 http://www.bowker.com/

Trust me. I know all this is adding up to a lot of money, but once your book is out…it's out there. For good.

Layout artist: $25/hr–$150/hr.

Unless you are a graphic artist by trade, **hire someone to do your cover**. $300-$2,500. The old cliché is a cliché for a reason. People DO judge a book by its cover.

Don't kid yourself.

Research your genre and see what other covers look like. (Side note: as much as I *LOVE* the covers of our YA books, and they are works of art, they turn off many teen readers. Some teens say the covers look too "young" for them. Avoid the pitfall that we fell into. Do your research.)

You own a professional publishing house now, so your books must look professional, *inside and out*.

TIPS FOR SAVING $$ ON PROFESSIONAL SERVICES

I know a lot of these figures can be scary, but remember that it doesn't all have to be done at once. Don't look at this and say "AHHHHH! This is going to cost me $50,000!"

This might be over a year's time. And, with a little bit of creativity, bartering, and possibly trade, you can get professional quality work for less. For example, college students learning their trade might do it for $15/hr rather than $100/hr. You get the quality. They get something for their resume. It's a win-win.

Many artists/freelance professionals will do work in trade or partial trade. Be creative. We got our GGC, the Geekalicious Gypsy Caravan, (normally a $6,000 job) designed and decorated for about $2,000 out-of-pocket.

The rest was in trade.

THE GEEKALICIOUS GYPSY CARAVAN (GGC)

Craigslist is a great place to find freelance artists and editors. It's where we found two of our cover artists Ia Esternä and James Koenig, and you see how gorgeous our covers are (pictured on following page). Just post an ad on Craigslist for an artist or cover artist. Be up front about how much you can pay. Then they can decide whether or not they can work within your budget before they even reply.

Do not offer a percentage of your sales. First of all it is an accounting nightmare, and you want to spend your time writing, not accounting. Secondly, as Dean Wesley Smith puts it, "Like giving the gardener a percentage of your house for trimming a hedge."[1] He is very outspoken on not paying day labor a percentage of your intellectual property. Their contribution is very important, and the analogy to the gardener isn't great, as having your book professionally edited and getting a professional book cover is far more important than having your hedges trimmed; but I see his point.

Hire an artist, editor, proofreader, and pay them what you can. Be up front about how much you can pay and that this is a work-for-hire situation, meaning they have no legal claim to the work afterwards. You own it. The contract must be a work-for-hire contract. Alternatively, for a piece of artwork, you can license the use of that art for use on your

---

1 Smith, Dean Wesley. "Paying for Self-Publishing Help." *The Writings and Opinions of Dean Wesley Smith.* 25 Mar. 2011. Web. 03 Apr. 2011.

book cover and the artist can still do whatever he/she wants with it. Make sure that the licensing term is "in perpetuity."

Now if you could find a single person, like an agent-turned-"estributor"[1] (as Konrath calls them), to do everything except the writing, that's editing, formatting, proofreading, book cover, uploading, etc., it might be worth the 15%; but they would have to do an excellent job, have professional connections, and do considerable maintenance and marketing work for it to be worthwhile for that 15%.

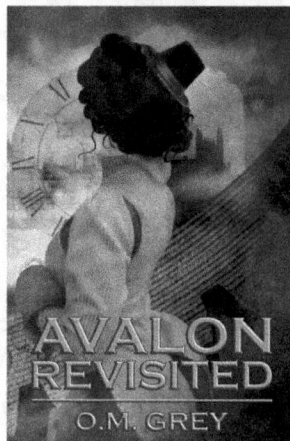

---

1 Konrath, J. A. "Ebooks and Self-Publishing - A Dialog Between Authors Barry Eisler and Joe Konrath." A Newbie's Guide to Publishing. 19 Mar. 2011. Web. 03 Apr. 2011.

CROWDSOURCING: RAISING MONEY FOR ART

In the past few years, crowdsourcing, like Kickstarter, IndieGoGo, and others, have become a very popular way for artists to raise money to produce their art. From musicians to filmmakers to fine artists to authors, crowdsourcing is a fabulous way to raise money to pay for professional services like cover art, editors, layout artists, and print runs.

I'm going to focus on Kickstarter, as it's by far the most popular platfrom, but I've had friends and colleagues raise thousands on IndieGoGo as well. The benefit of IndieGoGo is that you get whatever money you raise, even if you don't make your goal. Not so with Kickstarter. If you don't hit your goal, you don't get a dime. It can be very disappointing.

Fortunately, when I ran a Kickstarter in 2011, I hit my goal. Barely. Thanks to the generosity of a few individuals, both of whom will be appearing in my next book as a result of their donations, I made my goal and then some. Even those those two gentlemen donated the most, every since donation counts! Even those that donate $2 or $5.

It adds up.

Kickstarter[2] is for creative endeavors, and they will follow up to see if you're using the money as intended. It works through offering incentives or "rewards" for patrons donations.

First, choose how much you want to raise. I chose my amount of $4,000 by adding up all the money I'd need for an editor, cover artist, print run, and shipping costs to fulfill the rewards. It's best to offer a range of price rewards, starting with something very low like $1.00-$10.00 for a PDF eBook of the book or a special "thank you" on your blog, for example. Have an extremely high reward of $5,000 for a private reading for you and 30 of their friends, or something similar. You likely won't get anyone donating at that level, but you never know! The magic happens in between these numbers.

My Kickstarter was called "Blood, Sex, & Cogs: Steamy Steampunk & More by Olivia Grey. Search it from their website to see how I used creative names for each reward level. Make it fun. It helps.

---

2 http://www.kickstarter.com/

Here are examples of rewards for an author's Kickstarter:

$10 - eBook

$15 - author-signed book

$30 - author-signed book + personal phone call from author

$50 - three author-signed books

$100 - mention in the acknowlegments + 3 books (many rewards offer one new thing on top of everything leading up to that point)

$200 - short story, with the patron as the protagonist (or antagonist, if they prefer) + mention in the acknowlegments + 3 books

$250 - dedication in front of novel + short story (et. al.)

$500 - cameo appearance in next novel + 3 books

$1,000 - fully developed character in next novel + 3 books

$2,500 - private party with author for up to 30 people, including an author-signed book for each

Then it's up to your marketing abilities, connections and networks, and creativity to get this Kickstarter in front of the right people. If you've done your job, outlined in the Marketing section, of building and cultivating relationships with your networks and fans, you will be successful.

Don't think that if you create the Kickstarter people will throw money at you. They won't. There will be a few people who just like contributing to Kickstarter, but most donations will come from your fans and networks.

Make your Kickstarter project page as interesting and you possibly can. Make a video. If you don't have the talent, learn or hire someone to help you.

You're asking for thousands of dollars, put some effort into it.

Once you're Kickstarter is funded, make good on your promises in a reasonable amount of time. I wrote five short stories in six weeks to get them to those who donated. Several of those short stories are now being published elsewhere as well.

Brilliant, really.

FINAL ADMINISTRATIVE NECESSITIES

If you want your book to be considered for library inclusion, you absolutely must get a Library of Congress Control Number (LCCN) or Cataloging In Publication (CIP) number for your book. Submit your book to the Library of Congress for an LCCN number. You cannot get CIP numbers for your book unless your publishing house publishes at least three different authors and its books are widely acquired by U.S. Libraries. This is a minor problem, but not an insurmountable one. At this level in your business, having a CIP number is not essential, but at least an LCCN number is required. It doesn't cost anything but a little time and frustrating navigation through the LoC website.

First set up an account at http://pcn.loc.gov. Approval can take up to two weeks. Once the account is set, submit your title to the program. Response time is usually a few days, never more than a week in my experience. You will have to send them a copy or two of your book once printed.

Next, copyright your book with the U.S. Copyright office. It's about $35. Visit http://www.copyright.gov/, and set up an account. Thanks to the digital revolution, you can copyright a work through their eCO site with an online PDF submission. Once you submit your title, pay the fee, and upload the manuscript. Note that it could take over two years to get your certificate of copyright. They are that backed up. No worries, though, as you don't need the certificate in hand to publish your book. Once you file it with the copyright office, your work is copyrighted and protected. The copyright should be under the author's name and listed as such with the copyright year on the appropriate page of your book.

Do not list the editor of the book on the copyright unless you want them to own a piece of your book. The "editor" field is for editors of anthologies and the like, not editors and proofreaders. They should be paid as work-for-hire.

DISTRIBUTION & PRINTING

It traditionally flows like this:

Author→Publisher→Printer→Wholesaler→Distributor→Retailer→Reader. There are a lot of middle men. This is why Amazon.com has upset the system so much by becoming a single middle man, replacing Wholesaler through Distributor, and in some cases everything between Author and Reader, especially with eBooks and CreateSpace.

To have your book available virtually everywhere books are sold, they must at least be in one of the two main wholesalers: Ingrams or Baker & Taylor. Baker & Taylor has a partnership program for small publishing houses. It costs around $300 to sign up for it, but I wouldn't advise this unless you choose not to go with Lightning Source or CreateSpace for printing and distribution, the two best options for self-publishing.

LIGHTNING SOURCE (LSI)

Lightning Source (LSI) is the "distribution arm" of Ingrams, the largest book wholesaler in the United States. If you go through Lightning Source, your book will be available in both Ingrams *and* Baker & Taylor. Plus, a cool thing about Lighting Source is that it's more than a distributor. It's a printer and distributor rolled into one, and it was the "self-publisher's" (or micro/indie publisher's) best friend until their split with Amazon in mid-2011[1]. It's still a viable option, especially if you want to sell in bookstores, but unless you plan on traveling extensively to bookstores across the country, organizing signings and promoting those in each place, most of your sales will be through Amazon.com. Then, CreateSpace (CS) is your best bet for that.

Still, LSI is a great resource, although now it benefits a multi-authored, royatlty-based publisher more than an author self-publishing his/her own books, since it does require a business entity, not to mention their new relationship with Amazon.com.

After you have set up your business and gotten your ISBNs, etc, you'll need to set up a publisher's account with Lightning Source. There is no cost to create an account.

---

1 Friedlander, Joel. "Amazon and Lightning Source: The End of an Era?" *The Book Designer.* 9 Sept. 2011. Web. 18 Feb. 2013.

Once you have your assigned LSI team,

1. Submit a new title, which costs about $125. Via LSI, you can download templates for your artist/cover designer to use for the exterior PDF files of your book. The cover template will include a barcode, so don't buy one from Bowker. You can even choose whether or not to have the price coded into the barcode, and it's all for free, all included in that $125.

TIP

Several times a year, LSI offers "Free Title Setup" promotions, where they waive the set up fees if you purchase at least 50 copies before a certain date. You can save even more money this way.

Keep your eye out for these.

---

2. Once these templates have been filled with your content, you'll convert them to PDF and upload them to LSI. It's $40 for each upload (part of the $125 set up fee, but it will cost $40 for each subsequent upload if you make changes to the interior or exterior/cover, that means each time you find a new typo. Believe me, you'll find a lot of typos, even after having it professionally edited).

3. Order a proof ($30 paperback, $35 hardcover) sent via FedEx straight to your door. If everything looks good in the proof, you're set!

Either choose to have your book available direct-to-publisher only, meaning that you can order them but they won't be available online, or for just $12 a year, choose to be included in the Lightning Source distribution system. Then your book will be *available* wherever books are sold, because they're now in both Ingrams and Baker & Taylor's system. By choosing this option, your titles are available from Amazon, Barnes & Noble, Independent Bookstores, etc.

> ### REALITY CHECK
> Being *available* doesn't mean bookstores like Barnes & Noble will *carry* your books on the shelf. That's a whole different ballgame. Being available means that bookstores can type in the author's name, ISBN, and/or book title in their system, and it will be available to order for the inquiring customer. It's still up to you to get the customers in the store asking for it.

Via LSI's distribution, your titles are automatically available from Amazon.com and BN.com (Barnes & Noble) online which is convenient since more and more people are buying books online. Most customers, I'd wager, buy online through Amazon,com, although there are those, especially Nook users, who are loyal to Barnes & Noble. With the LSI/Amazon split in 2011, your LSI books will still be available through Amazon.com, but they are no longer stocked by Amazon.com. Often, when a consumer gets to your LSI fed Amazon.com title, it *could* read "usually ships in 1 to 3 weeks," which is the immediate death of that sale. That mixed with the higher per-book cost over CreateSpace, not to mention CreateSpace's free setup and revisions, made me turn away from Lightning Source as my printing/distribution choice.

One of the other great things about Lightning Source (and CreateSpace) is that they are a POD (Print On-Demand) printer, which means your book isn't printed until it's ordered. This is a HUGE thing in today's market. I'm a lifelong environmentalist, so this makes perfect sense to me.

Even some Big Boys are in trouble because of the excessive book printing (100,000+ print runs) vs. bookstore returns. Not to mention warehouse space costs, etc. Ultimately, books get thrown away (not even recycled in many cases), so POD is a no-brainer for me.

With LSI, they're printed and shipped as they're ordered within 24 hours.

They're never unavailable through Amazon, although they might be delayed as mentioned above, or any other bookseller, which as I mentioned before happened to us with our first indie publisher.

In the middle of a nationwide book tour our books were unavailable.

Not good. Never again will I be in the middle of a huge promotional push and have my books unavailable. Although "selling out" looks really good in a press release, it really means loss of potential sales.

> ## REALITY CHECK
> Having your book available wherever books are sold is not the same thing as bookstores stocking your books. I know I just said this, but it is important enough to repeat.

People are impulse buyers. Only a small percentage will come back to buy something that wasn't there when they wanted to purchase. Make sure your book is always available for your potential readers.

As a micro/indie publisher, Lightning Source is one way to go, but I recommend at least starting with CreateSpace as a self-published author. Read on to see why.

AMAZON'S CREATESPACE

Amazon's CreateSpace (CS) has become my #1 recommended resource for self-publishers and even micro/small publishers. There are several indie publishers who publish at least ten different authors that are now going the CS route as well.

Since Amazon's split with LSI[1], coupled with CSs free and easy set up, their professional product, and their distribution through the largest worldwide bookseller, CreateSpace has become the self-publisher's dream. Amazon, as you will read all about in the Marketing section of this book, is good to authors. There aren't many in this industry looking out for the author, but Amazon.com is one them. Don't get me wrong,

---

1 Sullivan, Robin. "CreateSpace Vs Lightning Source." Write to Publish. 14 July 2011. Web. 18 Feb. 2013.

they make tons of money on being good to the author, so it behooves them to do so. Unlike other publishers and distributors, they have not yet sacrificed the rights and success of their authors for a few more cents, knowing, in the long run, it will only hurt their bottom line, not help it.

In the first edition of this book, I coupled CS in with LuLu as LSI-light and being on-the-fence of a vanity press, since they used to be BookSurge, but now both CS and LuLu have improved in both quality and distribution. CreateSpace is now a proper POD printer and distributor rolled into one, and it's free, for the most part.

Unlike LSI, there is no set-up fee. Anyone can publish through CS, so you don't need a publishing company. This can be a viable option if you're just experimenting with self-publishing and just plan on publishing one or two books in print or if you plan to have a dozen or more books in print.

CreateSpace works well in conjunction with Amazon's KDP Kindle publishing service (more in the eBook section). However, there are some limitations in comparison to LSI. Your book will be available for purchase, in stock, on Amazon.com, but it will not be available through other channels without additional fees. These fees are minimal, especially considering you just saved $125 on set up fees. Plus, there is no cost for interior/exterior updates.

In the first edition, one of the many reasons I recommended LSI over CS was the difference in the per-book cost for printing. That, too, has changed. Whereas a 240 page 8.5x5.5 paperback from CS did cost $6.30 to LSI's $4.50 two years ago, that price has dropped to $3.85 per book through CS and has raised to $6.06 through LSI (including a $1.50 handling fee). LuLu is still at a whopping $8.75 per book, plus they don't even have the 8.5x5.5 size, nor the 8x5 size, my favorite.

Even if you do a small bulk order at 300 units, the LSI price drops to $3.42 per book while CS remains at $3.85 per book. You do not get bulk discounts through CS like you do through LSI and LuLu, but even LuLu's bulk discounts are outrageous with a per-unit cost of $7.00 each at 300.

LuLu, as far as I'm concerned, is out of the running at this point for self-published authors. I'll talk more about LuLu in the vanity press section and outline what the few good things are about them as a publishing choice, and I mean FEW.

For CS's Expanded Distribution Channel (EDC), makes your book available through Ingrams and Baker & Taylor, just like LSI. Upgrade your account for the $25 and go with the EDC. It's well worth it, even though the bulk of your sales will be through Amazon.com. With the EDC, your book will be available via Amazon.com in the US and Europe, bookstores and other online retailers like Barnes & Noble, and even in libraries and academic institutions (if you use a CS-assigned ISBN). Your earned royalties are somewhat less through expanded distribution, but that's because these other places must buy them at the 55% industry standard discount.

Through CS, you get higher royalties than through any traditional publisher or through LSI self-publishing. Whereas $1.00 per book was about as high as any royalty was before, much higher than through a traditional publisher, through CS, you can maximize your royalties with direct sales through Amazon.com, which, as I've said multiple times, will account for most of your online and offline sales unless you travel extensively and do events. A 240-page 5.5"x8.5" paperback priced at $12.95 (again, a little high for that size) would earn $1.45 through CS expanded distribution and $4.04 through Amazon.com sales. Priced the same through LSI, with a 55% standard discount, you'd earn a $1.26 royalty per book (with printing at $4.56 each) through Amazon or any other outlet. However, you can choose the minimum 20% discount, and although that will not work for Barnes & Noble, Amazon will still buy them at that price. The minimum 20% discount bumps your royalty up to $5.80 per book sold! Even better than that $4.04 though CS; however, remember what I said about that pesky little "ships 1 to 3 weeks" caveat that's possible with LSI and the hefty set-up fees. Hmmmm.

Do your research.

The CS royalty calculations are intricate, but you can read all about them through createspace.com[1]. Amazon.com is very good at making explanations, algorithms, sales, and calculations[2] accessible to the author.

Amazon's CreateSpace[3] has far surpassed LSI for the preferred printer/distributor of independent authors and publishers. CS's distribution is as extensive as LSI's, even though you'll soon find out that at this stage of the game that isn't even necessary. Unless you can get in with a major distributor, your books will not be on the bookshelves of bookstores, meaning the only way people will find out about your book as a self-published author is through your own marketing efforts.

One author described CS as Etsy for authors. A great choice for the independent author, self-published author with his/her own publishing company, and the micro/small indie publisher, CreateSpace is the best choice for mostly internet and eBook sales, which is where 99% of your sales will be.

Through CS, you don't have to use an ISBN, but at the same time, you can provide your own ISBN and imprint! CreateSpace, like their parent company Amazon.com, have bridged the gap for the independent author and small publishing company, alike. They offer everyone, from an author publishing a single book with no business entity to a place for self-published authors with a publishing company to even micro/small presses, an affordable place to print their books without sacrificing quality and the means to distribute them widely.

SUBMISSION INTO BOOKSTORES

Every major chain has their own submission process, but I'm going to focus on Barnes & Noble, especially since their greatest brick-and-mortar rival, Borders, is now defunct. Barnes & Noble is my favorite of the large chain stores, both as a consumer and as an indie author. They

---

1 https://www.createspace.com/Products/Book/Royalties.jsp
2 https://www.createspace.com/Products/Book/#content6:royaltyCalculator
3 Read this personal account of an indie author working with CreateSpace: http://www.boingboing.net/2011/04/04/diy-publishing-getti.html

were pretty great to us for signings, and they normally give you a free Starbucks during your author signing. Can't beat a free mocha!

First thing you simply must do if you want *ANY* bookstore to carry your book is to make your book RETURNABLE.

This sucks. I know. But it's currently part of the rules of this ridiculous game. Again, it's part of the reason why even the Big Boys are in dire straits right now.

Everything is returnable back to the publisher.

Think if you had 100,000 copies printed and only 25,000 copies sold. Everything else was returned.

That's a lot of returns.

That's a lot of lost money.

If you want to do bookstore signings at Barnes & Noble, you must make your book RETURNABLE if you set up your title through Lightning Source. You can choose to have LSI either destroy the returned books or ship them to you. Either way, as the publisher, you're paying for the returns. It comes out of your income/royalties from LSI.

Not only do you have to make it returnable through LSI, it has to also be at a 55% discount to the bookstores. Again, this sucks; but it's the industry standard, so it's necessary if you want bookstores to carry your title(s).

Once it shows up in Ingrams's database as returnable with at least a 55% discount, you're ready to go. (Give it a few weeks to be sure.)

Then you (as the publisher) must send two finished books, a letter of intent, and a detailed marketing plan to:

Diane Simowski
Small Press Dept.
Barnes & Noble, Inc.
122 Fifth Avenue
New York, NY 10011

Then, cross your fingers. If you did your job by hiring a good editor, cover artist, layout designer, etc., and the quality of writing and visual presentation is up-to-industry-par, then there is no reason for Barnes & Noble not to carry your book in their warehouse.

> ### REALITY CHECK
> This still doesn't mean it's on the shelves in every bookstore, though. It means that B&N can get them faster, since they're in their own warehouse, and that you can do book signings in their stores, the single best way as a micro/indie publisher to GET BOOKS ON THE SHELF.
> It is a lot of work and a lot of travel.

When you do a signing, Barnes & Noble will over-buy because they know they can return what doesn't sell.

Yes, you pay for any returns.

But returning them to their own warehouse rather than to LSI means that another Barnes & Noble can then carry them, so they're not returned to LSI right away.

Shelf space is precious. Barnes & Noble carries millions of books in the database, but any given store only has room for about 100,000. Much of this shelf space is occupied by bestsellers, classics, and publisher-purchased space.

That's right, major publishers buy bookstore real estate.

How do the NYBBs get so many of their books on the bookstore shelves? Big Boys have two things you don't:

1.   Sales Representatives that negotiate huge purchases for a title or several titles from their catalog with B&N Corporate in NYC.
2.   Deep pockets to pay for good bookstore placement.

Oh yeah. They pay for it. They pay BIG for it.

You know that table in every Barnes & Noble that says "New in Paperback?"

Publishers **PAY BIG BUCKS** to have their books on that table. Same goes for "New Releases," certainly not every one of the 950 books published on a given day will be on that shelf. Nope. Only the ones that PAY to be there. And B&N Corporate won't even talk to a small publisher about buying bookshelf space.

Same goes for end caps, the end of the bookshelves lining the aisles.

Authors of the Month, February 2009
Austin-area Barnes & Nobles

Publishers pay big because they know that the majority of brick-and-mortar shoppers find their next book due to bookstore placement.

Period.

You simply cannot compete with that. This is part of the "cons" of being "self-published" or going with an indie publisher.

The only prominent display in B&N that's not paid for is the "Bookseller Recommends" section. If you can get in good with one of the booksellers, perhaps they'll "recommend" your book. So be friendly and personable and use those networking skills when you do your book signings, perhaps an employee will put your book in that coveted section.

As mentioned above, there is another way to get your book on their bookshelves and that is to have a book signing there. If the CRM (Community Relations Manager) is worth their salt, they'll have posters in the window leading up to your event, a display of your books before and after you're there, and you'll be mentioned in the calendar (both in-store and on the internet). Likely your books will be returned after about a month, but that is still a month of shelf space surrounding an event. If you're really lucky, they'll keep a copy or two on hand.

Ethan and I have done about 100 Barnes & Noble book signings from coast-to-coast. About 30% of the CRMs really, truly cared and did their job extremely well, which means a successful signing for you and for them. About 40% were just going through the motions, and the final 30% weren't even there on the night of our signing. So, obviously they didn't care.

We kept a list.

As for Independent Bookstores, many of them will deal directly with the publisher (i.e., you) on consignment or wholesale. Get to know your local booksellers. We had the honor of being authors of the month at all Austin-area Barnes & Nobles.

You can't pay for publicity like that.

Also check out IndieBound[1] for a list of Independent Bookstores nationwide. This is even more work because there isn't a central office or uniform process.

Have I mentioned that a day job is much less stress, much less work, and a steady paycheck? I did mention that, right?

All of this said, as a "self-published" author, bookstores will not be your major outlet for selling books. The cost is very high and the return is very low. You will have much higher ROI[2] by marketing online.

Which brings us to your other best friends: Amazon and The internet, both will be covered extensively in the Marketing section.

We've actually stopped making our books returnable, as most of our sales were made in person or online. After the first year of sales via bookstores and bookstore signings, we ended up paying nearly twice as much in returns[3] as we received in "royalties" via LSI.

Not good.

Because, as in all royalties, you get a small percentage. When a bookstore buys a book from Ingrams/Baker & Taylor, they are paying the 55% discount, which is a few dollars more than the print cost. Those few dollars are your "royalty."

Now, when the bookstores return unsold books, the publisher not only has to give back those few dollars per book, they also have to pay for the printing of the book and the shipping. So, per book, you get about $1.50 in royalties, but for returns you pay $7.00 (returned royalty, print cost, shipping). One return ate up the royalties for nearly 5 books.

TIP
Put all "royalties" from LSI in a separate account. Use this money to pay for returns.

---

1 http://www.indiebound.org/
2 ROI = return on investment
3 These are returns from bookstores, not readers

This is the price for having your books on the shelf. High price to pay, and you will have to decide for yourself if it's worth it.

Even if you choose to make your book nonreturnable, they are still *available* in Barnes & Nobles and other bookstores, but a customer requiring will have to prepay for the book before the bookstore will order it. The customer will likely just purchase it through Amazon.com or BN.com.

If you decide to print with LSI, my advice is to forget bookstore marketing for awhile. Don't make your titles returnable and choose the minimum 20% discount. Your titles will still be available through Barnes & Noble, et al., but you will get more per title. Remember, only about 1% of your sales will be through this channel.

MANDATORY RETURNS
"Mandatory Returns & Kindle"

Back in November 2008, we had a great book signing at the Borders in Collin Creek Mall (Plano, TX). We sold 13 books! Whereas most emerging authors sell an average of one to five books at a bookstore signing, 13 is pretty great!

Over the holidays the following month, I found myself back at Collin Creek Mall for some shopping with my mother, so we thought we'd stop by and see how the sales were going. The woman, who was so friendly and helpful the day of our signing, was rude and short with us.

"They're in the back, set to be returned," she said, frowning.

I asked her if any others had sold since we left.

"A few," she replied vaguely.

"Then why are they being returned?" I asked, puzzled, since my understanding was that books were returned only if they weren't selling.

"They're on a mandatory return list."

HUH?!?!?! What on earth is a mandatory return list? I couldn't get anything else out of the woman. My mother assured me her rudeness was due to her embarrassment of having to face the author with this bizarre news, but *still*! Mandatory Return List?!!!

I haven't been able to find out much about Mandatory Return Lists, but I do know that books of all kinds are returned on a regular basis, even best selling phenomenons like *Twilight* and *Harry Potter*. It seems that bookstores basically sell books on consignment. They order A LOT from the wholesaler, who in turn gets their books from the distributor, who gets them from the publisher, who is responsible for printing the books. The bookstore gets a refund from the wholesalers. The wholesaler gets a refund from the distributor. The distributor gets a refund from the publisher, and the publisher eats the cost of the printing.

This is why so many independent publishers have such a rough time. Even the Big Boys in New York are feeling it. According to Richard Curtis, "the consignment system of selling books is bleeding the publishing industry to death."[1]

Those returned books ultimately go into the trash...yes, the trash–probably not even the recycling bin. As a long standing environmentalist, all I can see are all of those dead trees. And for what? Bookstores over-order because they know they can return

---

1 Curtis, Richard. "Behind Publishing's Wednesday of the Long Knives." eReads. 04 Dec. 2008. Web. 07 Apr. 2011.

them. The bookstores don't lose. Publishers do. Ultimately, authors (and the trees) do.

Although "on-demand-publishing" is still synonymous with "self-publishing," which still has a stigma attached to it, Curtis believes that this, and digital eBooks, like those one can read on Kindle, is the way of the future. Kindle, like the Sony Reader and others, is a digital eBook reader. According to Amazon, the screen reads like the pages of a book rather than a computer screen, so it's easier on the eyes. Amazon sold out of this amazing Kindle weeks before Christmas. It was touted as the Number One Christmas gift. Ebay and other such places were price gouging, asking as much as $1,000 for a normally-priced $360 Kindle.

I totally want a Kindle! After having moved across the continent more than a couple of times, moving thousands of books is a huge undertaking–*they're heavy*! Sure, I still want my fancy, old book collection. There are some books that I want to feel in my hands and smell the pages, etc…but, really, how many books do we all read that we LOVE that much? Most books pass the time and entertain us for a few hours or days, but they don't really change our lives.

My recommendation: buy books on a Kindle (or some such device) first. If you love it that much, then it's worth the extra $10-20 to get it for your bookshelf. Of course, we're confident that you'll love our book that much.

Come get an author-signed copy and check us out On The Road…where we'll be promoting *Rowan of the Wood* and trying to wipe out Mandatory Return Lists.

(Published on C&E blog[1], January 7, 2009)

Since writing that blog post over four years ago, I've learned that Barnes & Noble also has a mandatory return list, and worse, they have books that are automatically ordered. It's a great gig if your book is on that list, but it won't be. Not if you're self-published or with an indie press. Maybe not even if you're with a NYBB. Automatically ordered means that, say *Hamlet*, needs to have at least three copies on the shelf. This is a number decided on by Barnes & Noble Corporate. When one *Hamlet* is sold, another one is automatically ordered.

Now take the Indie or "self-publisher." You do all I recommended above and get your books on the Barnes & Noble shelves. In a month, you sell through. That's it. Your book is not on the list to be automatically reordered, so even though you may have sold twenty copies in a few weeks, your book will not be reordered.

Flawed system. Most definitely, but that is the only system we have to work with for the moment.

Despite all the ins and outs of the publishing/distribution world, as a "self-publisher," Lightning Source (LSI) or CreateSpace (CS) is the best way to go because you get quality printing and extensive distribution in one[2]. If you choose to go with another printer, you will have to find your own distribution. This could work for you. Perhaps the distributor you find will have sales representatives who have relationships with book stores and can actually get your book on the shelves. However, unless you have a multi-author house, a proven track record, and a thorough business/marketing plan, it will be difficult to find a distributor on your own. It certainly can be done, but at this point you must ask yourself if you are more interested in being a publisher or an author. "Self-publishing" via LSI or CS is time consuming enough. Going this other route will be infinitely more.

Again, it depends on your goals.

---

2 Neither Lightning Source nor Amazon is paying me to say these things. (Although they should!) I have just been very pleased with their services and quality.

AUTHOR CO-OP

Since early 2010, we've been experimenting with a new business model, and it's proving to be quite successful. This type of business is further bridging the gap between "self-publishing" and "indie publishing." An author co-op had the best of both models.

With an author co-op, each author keeps control of their own rights and each can save thousands by teaming up with other authors/artists for things like editing, cover design, book layout, and more.

The idea is to get a group of authors with similar goals: they all want to self-publish and be proactive with their writing careers. The beauty of author co-ops is that the "self-publishing" aspect is veiled to the public, since the publisher has more than one author and an umbrella imprint.

We've set up our author co-op under an LLC[1] because it was already established, so we take care of maintaining the LLC; however, if you're creating a company from scratch, you can pool money and talent together to set up the legal entity first. If this is the case, each author can initially buy into the co-op for a relatively small fee. Each participating author would sign a contract or deal memo ensuring that each will retain the rights and liabilities to their original work. Be sure to include a clause that all legal responsibility falls on the author (including, but not limited to, suits claiming copyright infringement and plagiarism), especially if you choose a sole-proprietorship or general partnership as your business structure.

Establish a group of authors who have complementary talents. Ideally, you all write well, as you want to be producing quality novels. But then one may have InDesign[2] and know how to use it. Another may be a whiz with Photoshop and cover/graphic design. Another may be good at editing and proofreading. Perhaps you will have non-authors in your group as well, like artists who want to have more of their work in the marketplace. You will have someone with a penchant for accounting and paperwork, etc. Then together you work toward a common goal.

---

1 Limited Liability Corporation, provides a protective layer between the owner and the sue-happy public.
2 Adobe software for desktop publishing and book layout. Another brand is QuarkXpress.

ADVICE

Even if you are forming a co-op with life-long friends, protect yourselves legally. Put it all in writing. It's the best way to remain friends. Memories tend to be selective.

Most of this work can be done in full or partial trade, or for just a small administrative fee. Everyone owns their own rights. Everyone gets their own royalties. As there is no such thing as a no-cost pass through, whomever is actually uploading files to LSI/CS and dealing with distributing checks, etc. should get a small percentage for their time. Blue Moose Press works under a 15% administrative fee or $20, whichever is less for said tasks.

Now your co-op can pool together money to buy a big block of ISBNs from Bowker. 100 ISBNs cost just under $600. Definitely the best way to go, unless you go for 1,000, which is $1,000. One dollar per ISBN is an incredible price. If your Author Co-op has ten authors or more, 1,000 could be the way to go. Your publishing house would have its own ISBN prefix.

Much like romantic relationships, each individual co-op needs to establish what will work best for their particular group. This could be as simple as an understanding between friends and colleagues or it could be something with by-laws and corporate regulations.

When your co-op publishes its books, put a list of other titles available by your publishing company at the end of each book. (See the end of this book for an example.)

Cross-promotion is gold.

Share the cost. Reap the benefits.

As I said at the beginning, it all depends upon what you want and what you're willing to risk and/or sacrifice.

That's what it really comes down to.

Know yourself.

Know your goals.

Make an informed decision.

"SELF-PUBLISHING" PROS & CONS

PROS

- You're the master/mistress of your own destiny.
- You keep all the rights to your story, characters, merchandising, film/TV, etc.
- You don't have to wait years to see your book in print or to have readers enjoying your work.
- You don't have to worry about someone preying on your dreams and taking advantage of you.
- If you do your job of publishing and marketing the book(s) well, then you might gain the attention of a NYBB. If they want to acquire your book, it's on your terms. You have some negotiating power. (Examples of this happening: *Eragon* series, *Diary of a Wimpy Kid, 50 Shades of Grey,* and countless others).
- Take it on the road, and you can make a modest living just selling your book at events (more in the marketing section).
- You meet your fans as you build readership <u>one-by-one</u>.

CONS

- You don't have the industry/media connections that you would with a Big Boy or even a large, well-established Independent Press.
- You have to do *everything* yourself or pay to have it subcontracted (or divvy up the tasks among the authors in the co-op)
- It is an unbelievable amount of work, and it becomes your life
- It's a constant struggle to be seen among the millions of other authors/books out there
- It's the second most expensive way to get your book published, in the short run, but it can turn out to be a great investment in the long run.
- It's an *extremely* slow process
- One....by....one....you build your readership

4. VANITY PRESS

(Subsidy Press, POD Publishing)

The last of the Four Basic Choices is vanity publishing. Normally when people say "self-publishing," they mean this, which is why I don't consider owning one's own publishing company as "self-publishing" **when talking to the public**. When talking to the people at events, I always say our books are published by an independent publisher, as it truly is. "Self-published" really means vanity publishing in most circles. Unfortunately, most people do not make the distinction. It is not truly self-published because the author is paying someone else to publish it.

I do not recommend the vanity press[1] option unless *you only want to see your book in print* and you plan to sell it/give it to a few friends and family or have as companion material for a seminar (or after some other performance, like poetry reading). Generally people will pay more than normal for something after they've seen a live performance of it, and it is quite literally impossible to price a vanity press published book to be comparable with others in the market.

In fact, forget what I just said. I can't even recommend it for those things anymore. Do not use a vanity press at all. Ever. End of story.

Do not pay ANYONE to publish your book.

Even if you only want to see your book in print and give it to a friend or two, sign a copy to mom and grandma, I'd still recommend CreateSpace over any vanity press like Xlibris or iUniverse.

STAY AWAY FROM THOSE!

Here's why: they charge you a minimum of $899 up front. Yep. That's before any printing costs. That's just for the priviledge of publishing your book. You will NEVER make that cost back through a vanity press like Xlibris or iUniverse because if your book has one of those two names on its spine, it screams *amateur*.

Seriously.

---

1 During a recent workshop, the presenter said that the term "vanity press" was out of fashion. That type of publisher is now referred to as a subsidy press or POD publishing. I use these terms interchangeably throughout this section. I continue to use "vanity press," as this is the term I learned first.

Plus, if you want to sell your book on Amazon or even direct to your fans after a speaking event, this is definitely not the way to go. You will price yourself out of the market by going this route because the fees to publish through them are high, and the printing costs are even higher.

Basically, vanity publishers operate by:

- Having the author pay the vanity publisher, sometimes called a POD publisher, (iUniverse, Xlibris, AuthorHouse, and countless others) to publish their book. Please note, a POD publisher is quite different than a POD printer. As things are changing so quickly in this industry, many terms used are confusing. Please do your research. Victoria Strauss wrote excellent article[1] on the difference between the two as well as the Pros and Cons of POD publishers for the SFWA website.

- Providing different packages that offer various services and include prices that range from a few hundred to several thousand.

- Taking care of (thereby owning) the ISBN, copyright, LCCN, etc.

- Distributing the book worldwide, meaning it's available via online stores and for order at bookstores, similar to the Lightning Source distribution.

- Offering higher-end packages that 'provide' author support, etc. Perhaps for another fee, they offer cover design, etc.

- Having you pay a pretty high price for each book through their POD publishing services, which makes the cover price of your book too high for your market.
    - ❑ Example: a 240 page 8.5×5.5 paperback book costs $3.42 each when you get 300 printed via Lightning Source and $7.00 each from LuLu. This is short-run printing.
    - ❑ Per book, the way Amazon and BN.com buys them, is $4.56 through LSI and $8.75 through LuLu.

1 Strauss, Victoria. "Print-On-Demand and Electronic Self-Publishing." Science Fiction & Fantasy Writers of America. 7 Mar 2001. Web. 03 Apr. 2011.

❏ To get just $1.00 for each book from LuLu sold through Amazon or BN.com[2], the cover price has to be nearly $17.95. Too much for a book that size at just a $1.00 to you!

❏ That same book can be priced at a more reasonable $12.95 if distributed through Lightning Source via your own publishing company or CreateSpace, and your royalty will be a little higher per book, plus the lower prices means more sales.

❏ (Don't kid yourself that you'll ever get more than $1-2 per book sold through any kind of distributor. $2 per book is HIGH! Via Big Boys, your royalty is under $1.00 per book, and in most cases, under $0.30 per book.)

❏ These printing prices are based on trade paperbacks. Hard cover books are considerably more, usually twice the price to print.

• Having you order your books directly from the vanity press.

• Taking no responsibility for marketing. You must market your book, as you do in all the other choices. It's always up to you to market your book, no matter what avenue you take.

Publishing via vanity press is by far the most expensive way to get your book published.

You might as well throw your money into the street.

Some authors claim they prefer LuLu to LSI or Amazon's CreateSpace for various reasons, and truly, to each his/her own. For me, a savvy business woman, it comes down to the price, the quality, and what they offer. Let's take for example a 240-page perfect-bound 5.5"x8.5" trade paperback, as I did in the last section, but it's so important, it's worth repeating.

Per book cost with LuLu $8.75, but they don't have the 8.5"x5.5" trim size. This is the price for either the 6"x9" or A5 size (5.833"x8.264")

Per book cost with CreateSpace $3.85

Per book cost with LSI $4.56 + $1.50 handling fee = $6.06

---

2 Remember, they get books at a 55% discount off the cover price.

None of these costs include shipping. If you buy in bulk with LuLu or LSI, that price goes down. No matter the number, with CreateSpace the per book price stays the same.

LuLu also has fewer binding/trim sizes than LSI or CreateSpace. Lulu does offer a dust jacket and hardback option, like LSI, as well as a full-color comic book option, but the costs per book are so astronomical ($19.50/ea for a 240-page hardcover and $25.00/ea for a 100-page graphic novel) that the cover price would, again, price it out of the market.

If you were to offer the industry standard discount off the cover price to retailers (55%), just to earn $1.00 per book, the LuLu book would have to be priced at $17.95, which is pricing a 240-page paperback novel out of its market. Most of these books are under $10. With the LSI or CreateSpace title, it can be priced around $12.95, which is still high, but it always will be when dealing with such small print runs.[1] You would be amazed at how much a difference that $3.00 makes to the consumer. Plus, when you factor shipping and other costs into the production of that book, the price goes up.

> **PERSONAL NOTE:**
> As an example of the kinds of "additional services" these POD publishers offer, I paid an editor advertised through LuLu to edit *Rowan of the Wood* (before it was picked up by the first publisher), and it came back full of grammatical errors that weren't there when I sent it! I stupidly didn't re-read it myself, thinking that it had just come back from a "professional" editor. It was quite embarrassing for the initial test run of the book, seeing as how I'm an English Professor and all. Ultimately, it just created more work for me. Yes. That editor certainly had a comma fetish. No doubt.

---

1 Only with off-set printing (ordering 1500+ copies) will the per-book print price start to drop below $3.50 per book.

The only benefit I see to publishing with LuLu is if you want to publish a very low run casewrapped hardback or a trade paperback size, as those option are not available with either CreateSpace or LSI. You'll be paying top-dollar for the printing, meaning your book will be over priced for its market. Perhaps a limited collector's edition hardback would be worth it. I think that would be the only reason I'd ever use LuLu again, and that would be after I exhausted every other option.

Do your homework.

Go to a few vanity press sites like those listed above and do the math, not only the short run on getting your book published, but in the long run of marketing and selling your book. Many of them have calculators on their site. Run the numbers for your particular scenario and see what makes sense. Just know and understand what you're signing up for, its benefits, and its limitations.

Having iUniverse or Xlibris or even LuLu as the imprint on the spine of your book screams amateur.

Seriously.

CreateSpace is my top recommendation. If you decide that it's the right publishing path for you, pay the extra money to get a custom ISBN or Custom Universal ISBN. Don't use CreateSpace as your imprint if you want to look professional.

As far as I know, no major chain bookstore carries books on the shelves from a vanity publisher, period. You *might* be able to get a book signing in a Barnes & Noble, although it's highly unlikely because you cannot make the books returnable, and they will unlikely keep them around afterward. But you can't get in a bookstore to begin with unless you have the option of making your books returnable through your vanity press.

There are, of course, as in anything, exceptions.

Be sure to define your goals and weigh your sacrifices/risks honestly with yourself before choosing a publishing route. Which road you take really depends upon this.

PART II: MARKETING

Marketing your book can be a full-time job. Period. You can put as much or as little into it as you like. The more you put into marketing your book, the more books you will sell; however, it is continuous work and the returns aren't what one would expect for such work. The road to a bestseller, or even a semi-known author, is a very, *very* long and arduous one.

Remember that this is a multi-year, multi-thousand dollar investment on your part. It takes time to build a readership, so don't burn yourself out in the first year, like I almost did. If you want to be a working[1] author, you are in this for the long haul. Pace yourself.

Even if you haven't finished your book yet, it's never too early to start planning and implementing your marketing plan. Start a blog, and update it at the very least once a week, three times is preferable. Build your Twitter and Facebook and Goodreads (et al.) communities. Get to know your community and allow them to get to know you. Do all of this now. You cannot start too early. Please do not wait until your book is out. You need these networks in place for your release. They need to know you, like you, and trust you first. Otherwise, you will appear to be just another person trying to sell them something, and people are really, really tired of that.

Marketing in our digital age is both easier and more difficult than ever. It's easier because of the number of inexpensive or free marketing

---

1 Heavy emphasis on "working."

avenues available to every single person. It is more difficult than ever due to the same reason. There is so much information crossing cyber-space every second, it's quite likely you will get lost in the shuffle.

In late February 2011, Publishers Weekly and Digital Book World hosted a web seminar titled "The Evolution of Self-Publishing." The following is an excerpt as reported by Publishers Weekly[1]:

> 'Authors really need to look at what their goals are and how they're going to realistically achieve them.' Carolyn Pittis, SVP, Global Author Services at HarperCollins, agreed: 'Marketing is the issue of our time. Book marketing is the biggest challenge that anyone in the book business is facing today, purely because there's so much noise and so much content getting created and so many potential distractions.' Marketing often determines a book's commercial success—or failure, said Phil Sexton, publisher and community leader at Writer's Digest. 'It's about what the intent of the author is. How much they're going to back [their book], whether or not they're going to try and sell it.'

It truly is about your own personal goals, your own personal strengths, and your own level of commitment. It is not an easy road. It is not a short road. But it can be an interesting and enjoyable drive.

THE FOUR MAXIMS OF MARKETING

Over the years, my marketing knowledge as an unknown author has been boiled down to four maxims. While reading through the rest of this section, please keep them in mind.

1. **People are BUSY.** Many families have multiple income sources and often times multiple jobs to make ends meet. This is in addition to kids, pets, paying bills, running errands, and just life in general. People are very busy. It is essential to keep this in mind when marketing your book. As an unknown author, people will rarely make time for you. Sure, they will make time to meet Stephen King or J. K. Rowling, but unknown, struggling

---

1 Adriani, Lynn. "Web Seminar Debates How Self-Publishing Will Lose Its Stigma." Publishers Weekly. 23 Feb. 2011. Web. 02 Apr. 2011.

authors are a dime a thousand. Make your marketing efforts simple and fast for them. Time is valuable.

2. **People are BROKE,** especially in today's economy. Just on my street alone, there are a dozen homes for sale, at least half are due to foreclosure. Our home was on the verge of foreclosure in 2009. We bought a new foreclosed home in California in 2012. They can no longer afford high priced items, which can be good news for a book, as it is relatively low-cost for hours of entertainment. Still, they may have a very tight budget when it comes to entertainment. If they only have $20 a month to budget for books, they will unlikely spend that $20 of it on an unknown author for a single book. This is where the vanity press option really hurts you. Why buy a 240 page book for $20 from an unknown author when they can buy a 240 page book for $8-10 from an author they know they like? Few people do.

3. **People are LAZY.** This is especially true when it comes to contests and things you are asking your readers/potential readers to do. People are tired from working all the time. They want a break. They want to play video games. They want to watch TV or Netflix. They don't want to be sold to on social networks or in bookstores, so you must make whatever you're asking of them so simple, that they literally just have to click their mouse once. **KISS.** *Keep It Simple. Seriously.* Even that one mouse click is often too much.

4. **Above all...it's a numbers game.** The more people you reach, the more will buy your book. The more eyes that see you, whether online or in person, the more will buy your book. In my online marketing experience, less than 10% of people reached will actually click that link, less than 1% of that 10% will actually make a purchase. If you only reach 100 people, don't expect to make a sale. If you reach 1,000, maybe one will buy your book. If you reach 1,000,000, then perhaps 1,000 will buy your book. These numbers are for online or distance sales, like articles, blog

posts, tweeting, advertising, etc. The numbers are different if the author is actually present. We've had people buy a book just to get an author-signed book. They never had an author-signed book before. As part of the Olivia experiment, discussed later in this section, I see the difference in the *Avalon Revisited* sales if I'm there as "Olivia" rather than Christine. If "Olivia" is there, *Avalon Revisited* sells better than if Christine is behind the table. Go figure. People want to meet the author. People really like author-signed books.

If you can find ways to reach and inspire people despite these four things, you'll be successful in marketing your book. Connect with them on a personal level. That is what it's all about.

SIX THINGS YOU'LL NEED TO MARKET YOUR BOOK

Before you start marketing your book, have these things at the ready. I keep them all together for each book in a single document organized by book title on my desktop, so I can easily open them and cut/paste into an online interview, email, query, submission, or guest blog post.

1. Author Bio.

You will use this more times than you realize. Have several, actually, in varying word counts. Write them up at 25, 50, 75, and 100-word blurbs. This should give a brief description of who you are and what you write.

Look at other author bios on the internet to get an idea of what to put in one. If you have the gift of humor, use that. I've read some very entertaining author bios that left me quite green, as I do not have that gift of wit. If your bio is fun, especially if the whimsy speaks to your writing style, then go for it. People like fun and witty. They respond well to it.

Just think, does anyone really care what university you attended? Unlikely. You're a writer. Be creative and fun with your bio. It is often the first thing a potential reader sees of you and your work.

You will be copying and pasting this bio so very often. Keep it handy.

DO THIS NOW.

You will be using this so much throughout your marketing, take the time and write these four lengths out now. I start with the longest, as I'm rather loquacious, and then trim, trim, trim until I get the other word lengths.

2. Author Picture.

Get a professional author picture taken. In fact, get several. These photos must look like you; i.e., no glamour shots. You want your readers to recognize you. Or perhaps you don't. The first author picture of my alter-ego/pen name didn't look anything like me, and the mystery behind it certainly generated interest. It was a fun (and ongoing) experiment. I've since altered my alter-ego to be more me, without the wig and bustle, but those Steampunk photos exist. This way, I can be recognized either way, as I slowly merge the two personas[1].

Make your picture interesting, unique. Let it speak to who you are.

3. Book Blurb.

Like your bio, you will need several short book blurbs describing your book. These are often harder to write than the book itself. Again, write them up in 25, 50, 75, and 100-word versions, as different places will ask for a specific word count. Best to have them all ready.

If you've already written your book, **DO THIS NOW**. If you haven't written your book or you're in the middle of your book **DO THIS NOW.** Sometimes it's easier to write these before the entire book is written or when it's just an idea. It's a great writing exercise in either case, and, of course, it can be revised at any time.

4. Marketing Materials.

These are bookmarks, fliers, etc. Get them professionally made. With digital technology, you can get high-quality printed bookmarks for just pennies each. It's well worth the effort.

I've been to author signings where the author handed me a business card printed out on their computer, with perforated edges. Bookmarks that are just on regular, flimsy printer paper and cut crookedly. Sometimes laminated. Sometimes not.

These things shout: AMATEUR.

---

1 Mollins, Julie. "Author creates second identity as O. M. Grey." Reuters. 18 August 2011. Web.

There are so many printing companies online that do this affordably. Take $50-100, and get some quality things made. I use NextDayFlyers. They're fast, their product is beautiful, and they're quite affordable. Their "club flyers" work out to $0.04 each when ordering 1,000 of them. If you don't have a talent for design, then find a friend who does or put an ad up on Craigslist for what you can pay or trade. Many artists and graphic designers are looking for work. Etsy is a brilliant resource for finding artists and reasonably priced marketing materials.

Your marketing materials should look professional. They should have your name, book cover, book blurb, website/blog, and links to your social networks. ISBN is optional, but it can be helpful.

Some authors make something called chapbooks to hand out or sell for a few dollars at events. This is a short saddle-stiched book containing excerpts from their novel or perhaps short stories and poetry. Normally sold for around $5.00, it could be something that later segues into a book sale. Be sure to have your contact information in the chapbook and where they can purchase your novel.

We've seen success with putting a flash fiction piece on one side of a postcard. The other side has all our networks, sites, and contact info. Quite effective, as the reader gets a taste of your writing style for free along with all the information on how to buy your books and find you onine.

5. Social Networking Sites.

Facebook. Twitter. Goodreads. LibraryThing. Pinterest. Tumblr. LinkedIn. GooglePlus. And others. There are so very many social networking sites, I can't keep up with them all, and I'm online almost constantly. It's too much to try to have a presence on all of them. Pick three or four, and work those. I'll be covering the two main ones, Facebook and Twitter, in greater detail shortly, and I'll also touch on Goodreads and Tumblr, briefly.

6. Blog/Website.

In today's marketplace, a blog/website is absolutely essential. The best way to get yourself a blog without extra cost and trouble is to go via a free blog service like WordPress or Blogger/Blogspot. I prefer WordPress because I find it easier to use, but the other services are just as viable.

This will be your marketing hub. Make it count.

YOUR BLOG CAN ALSO BE YOUR WEBSITE

You can build an entire website around one of these free sites hosted by WordPress or Blogger/Blogspot. In fact, I recommend it. No domain names to purchase. No web hosting service. No need to know HTML or use any WYSIWYG[1] editor to create a website. Plus it will give you an OpenID, which is simplifying logins on many sites. Instead of remembering a multitude of username/passwords, you can just sign in using your OpenID. An increasing number of sites will even let you sign in with Facebook or Twitter. It's all becoming rather integrated.

We have websites using both methods: traditional hosted websites with domain names and free WordPress blogs. I find the WordPress (blogs) route by far the best, and here is why:

- With WordPress, you have analytics built right into the dashboard. This means that you can see how many visitors visit your blog each day and how a particular post might have affected your numbers. You can see what search terms they used to find you. If you're consistently seeing higher numbers surrounding a certain type of post or subject, you can write similar posts and grow your readership. If you tweeted something one day or if a more visible author retweeted (RT'd) or included you in a #FF or #WW (explained in the Twitter section) and you received more hits than normal, you will know why through the built-in dashboard analytics. Powerful marketing tool. And it's free.

- You can set your blog up to post directly to Twitter and Facebook (and Tumblr, GooglePlus, LinkedIn, and others) as soon as you hit "publish" on your new blog post. You also have the ability to schedule future posts, which is essential if you need to do most of your marketing on one day but need content posted throughout the week. Getting as much of your online marketing as possible set up for automation is crucial if you are to have any time to write.

---

1 WYSIWYG = What You See Is What You Get, a type of user-friendly HTML editor

- If you truly must have your own domain name, then you can register for one and have it forwarded to your blog. You can even register for one right through WordPress, and it reminds you of that fact every day. In today's online communities, blogs are very respected. A simple authorsname.wordpress.com is a perfect way to have an online presence without the hassle. Without the cost. Once you're making the big bucks and are getting tens of thousands of hits a week, then you can think about getting a traditional website.

- When choosing your theme, the way your blog will look, be sure you have at least two columns and the theme is widget enabled. You will be using these "widgets," things you put in the sidebar(s), to cross-promote with Facebook, Twitter, Goodreads, etc., as well as have links to buy your books on Amazon. Always use your Amazon Associate link, another thing to have handy on your desktop, explained in the eBook & Amazon section.

TRADITIONAL WEBSITE

If you decide to go the route of a traditional website, you will likely have to hire someone to design the site for you, unless you have a background in web design. This can run anywhere from $200 to $2,000 or more. There is a way to host WordPress on your server and build a website around that, but you will not have the built-in analytics as stated above.[1] You will, however, be able to post fancy framed <iframe> content[2], like Amazon Associate ads, whereas you cannot do so on a free WordPress site. There you must post the link only. I'll go into this in more detail when I discuss Amazon at length later in the book.

With a traditional website you will have to register and pay for a domain name. This isn't expensive, but it becomes a hassle to renew them year after year, especially if you have more than one. A domain

---

1 In this case, use Google Analytics. There is also a WordPress plugin that works in tandem with this, enabling you to view the figures right on your WordPress dashboard.
2 <iframe> = fancy displays generated by Amazon's Associates program. When signed into your Amazon Affiliate account, click "Link to this page" in the top toolbar to get the code. The Amazon Associates program is explained later in the eBook section.

name is this: http://www.yourname.com. It costs anywhere from $7 to $30 a year, depending on the service you use.

With a traditional website, you will also have to pay for web hosting to hold your web files. Again, unless you are very internet savvy and are familiar with FTP sites, HTML, etc., this can get very complicated. Yearly web hosting is available for around $100/year.

Find out how many people are visiting your site by signing up for Google Analytics, a free service. They will have you paste a specific HTML code on your home page and any other page you wish to track. Again, more complicated than the built-in analytics on WordPress or Blogger, but useful just the same. You really must have a way to track your online visitors to ensure that your marketing outreach is effective.

Traditional websites, while potentially unique, are a lot of work to maintain. If you're getting less than 100 hits a week, it's just not worth the time to manage and update all of the files via FTP, especially if you have to pay someone to do it. You can have the same amount of hits on a free blog without the maintenance.

Take a look at our traditional websites:

http://www.christineandethanrose.com

http://www.rowanofthewood.com

They are quite beautiful; however, they are more difficult to maintain and, even with the hosted, integrated blog, have very few weekly visits.

Now look at our free WordPress blogs:

http://christinerose.wordpress.com

http://ethanorose.wordpress.com

http://omgrey.wordpress.com

By the end of the first month, there were more visits every day to the christinerose.wordpress.com site than the christineandethanrose.com site received in an entire month.

After blogging regularly on http://omgrey.wordpress.com for the past two years, that site averages 350-500 views every day. That's a huge difference from the 12 views I'd get on a good day for http://www.rowanofthewood.com.

Why? SEO.[1] Fresh content. Getting to know the author personally.

Ultimately, I will switch the above domain names to go directly to my free WordPress blogs, streamlining and simplifying even further.

Remember, even if you have the most beautiful website on the internet, it doesn't mean that you will have the visitors. You, your book, and your website/blog are a grain of sand on a mile-long beach.

It's difficult to be seen, but not impossible.

The following pages will help teach you how to be seen.

MARKETING STRATEGY

1. Start Local

Truly, there is no better place to niche market than in and around your home. Libraries and bookstores love local authors. So get known locally first, becoming that proverbial big fish, and then expand outward from there. Additionally, you will be able to continue working your current day job and/or writing full time to ultimately increase your visibility (because as readers discover you and fall in love with your work, they will want more. Have more ready).

We did the exact opposite of this in the GGC,[2] and paid dearly for it. Quite literally. It is very expensive to travel across the country, and although the theory was logical, it wasn't realistic. I naïvely thought that if we traveled far and wide, we'd establish a strong readership base who would then seek out the second book, third book, etc. I built up a newsletter list and stayed in contact with my readers, and the readers loved the book. However, ultimately marketing cards get lost and newsletter emails go unread, lost down people's ever-full inbox.

Remember Marketing Maxim #1: People are Busy.

As I discovered, our growing fan base would look for us at the same event the following year, and at the ones we returned to, we sold a lot

---

1 SEO = Search Engine Optimization, process of improving a websites visibility in search engines
2 The Geekalicious Gypsy Caravan, in case you've forgotten.

of sequels; but we couldn't afford to go as far or wide as we did the first year, so we missed out on a lot of sales.

Now we stay fairly local, and we're already seeing the benefit. For events now, we rarely travel more than eight driving hours, sixteen at the outset, and those are for very special events only (like where we're a GOH[3] or it's a known money-maker like the Colorado Irish Festival). Now fans are recognizing us, and because they see us in so many places, they begin to trust us as reliable and legitimate authors.

Start local. Build up from there. It's the wiser and more financially stable way to proceed. After all, you will be doing this for years, maybe the rest of your life.

Pace yourself.

2. Network & Don't Quit Your Day Job

Do as much as you can from home and near home. When you hear the clichéd advice "don't quit your day job," it's not because you or your book isn't good enough; it's for your own sanity. By keeping your day job, you eliminate the urgency and stress of trying to make ends meet, pay the mortgage, keep the lights and internet on, buy food and mochas. You are forced to start slowly, because no matter how intensely you market, it still takes time to build a BRAND, to build your name. More time that I'd like to admit, but that is the reality of it.

If you have a corporate job, you can write such great prose during those boring corporate meetings! Plus, you have a plethora of life experiences and dramatic fodder to put into your stories.

3. Pen Names

If you're a bit shy and an introvert, like many authors are, create a pen name and an entire persona to go behind it. I have found Olivia wonderfully liberating. I talk about things through Olivia's blog that I would never talk about on my own blog. I censor myself more as Christine Rose than I do as O. M. Grey, which is ironic since Olivia started out mysterious and aloof as a marketing experiment. She has since become more well-known and prolific than Christine Rose.

---

3 GOH = Guest of Honor

Or, if you feel you ruined your career as a writer because of some burned bridge, you can have a fresh start with a pen name.

Truly. Lots of fun, pen names.

However, I must recommend either/or. Don't try to maintain both, like I have. It's exhausting, and one persona will get more attention than the other due to time and energy constraints. Choose an author name, whether yours or a pen name, and stick with that.

Period.

4. O. M. Grey Experiment

After Ethan and I had traveled 19,000 miles, spent $65,000, and sold nearly 3,000 books our first major marketing year in 2009, we dipped into our savings to get the first and second book printed by an off-set printer. By going off-set as opposed to POD, we got cheaper per-book printing costs, but we had to buy at least 1500 copies to get that price. After all, we sold nearly 3,000 of the first book in the first year, surely we'll sell that many of the sequel! So those 3,000 books (1,500 of the first and 1,500 of the second) would last us, maybe, until the following summer.

I truly must laugh at this last statement to avoid crying.

Pile on top of that the failing economy and us nearly losing our house, long story, we found ourselves facing our second year with no savings and piling bills. AND I had just turned FORTY.

Really? I thought the universe had it out for me.

Turns out, one of the basic rules of publishing is that the sequel rarely sells as well as the first book. To this day, even with a third and fourth book out, we still sell far more of the first book than any of the sequels.

Secondly, we didn't travel nearly as much the second, third, or fourth year, so we didn't sell as many of the books. So three years after we bought that huge bulk of books, we still have half of them sitting in our house.

Reality sucks.

Enter Olivia (O. M.) Grey. Partly due to my disappointment and depression, I had the idea to do a marketing experiment. From my research into trying to find an agent in 2009, I knew that they were all looking for something called "Steampunk." During that time I looked into what that was, and it was way cool. That mixed with the popular genre of paranormal romance, thanks to *Twilight*, *True Blood*, and others, I had my mashup genre. For years I had wanted to put Arthur Tudor, older brother to King Henry VIII, in a story as a vampire, so I took my chance with this experiment.

I broke all the rules. ***ALL THE RULES.*** And, most importantly, I had a lot fun. I wrote the book I wanted to write. I didn't have to sensor myself because it wasn't "Christine Rose" writing it. I could be as dark and demented and debaucherous as I wanted to be, and I was. I let all my darkness and depression out on those pages. I wrote the first draft of what was to become *Avalon Revisited* in a month.

I created a Twitter account, a Facebook Fan Page, and a free WordPress blog for Ms. Grey. My motto for "Olivia" was to keep it as simple as possible. I was going to do the exact opposite of what I did as "Christine." Whereas Christine was everywhere, all the time–YouTube, Twitter, Facebook, BlogTalkRadio, BlogTV, Goodreads, etc. etc. etc.– Olivia was going to keep it simple and focused.

I took a picture of myself with my webcam wearing a top hat with some goggles on the brim. No one could see my face. You couldn't even tell if I was male or female. The username on all social networks was OMGREY, and don't think the OMG part was an accident either.

With the Steampunk elements in the book, I zeroed in on the Steampunk culture. Using TweetAdder (explained in the Twitter section), I followed tweets who either were talking about Steampunk or had the word Steampunk in their profile. I tweeted about Steampunk articles (see how to automate using Twitter, Google Alerts, and TwitterFeed below in the Twitter section).

Over the next two months, I revised the book, got it professionally edited, and hired a cover artist to make a cover comparable to that which was on the shelves, but including Steampunk elements. Once the cover art was complete, I got it up on my Twitter background (back before "new" Twitter, when users could still see a customized background), my blog, and my Facebook Fan Page.

Avalon Revisited was within three weeks of being released. It was already at the printer, and I was busy setting up a very small blog tour.

Then one day, a day just like any other, I got a tweet from Louise Fury, a literary agent. Turns out, she was intrigued by the strange picture of the top hat and goggles, so she visited my Twitter profile. There she saw the beautiful cover art and loved it, so she went to my blog. There she read the premise of the book, and she loved it. She DM'd[1] me and asked who my agent was. I, of course, didn't have an agent. I had given up on New York, as previously explained, but here was an agent knocking on my door.

She asked if I had anything else she could look at, and I told her the rights were available for *Avalon Revisited*, as I was on the verge of publishing it through "Christine's" publishing co-op, Blue Moose Press.

Louise asked for the first three chapters. Within the hour, she wrote telling me how much she loved it, and asked for the entire book, which she also devoured. By the end of the day, after consulting with her colleagues at the L. Perkins Agency, she offered me representation.

I said yes.

I went and danced in the middle of the street.

Seeing as how the book was only 55,000 words, way too short for a NY published romance, I would have to increase it by another 15-20K. New York, remember, needs to put it in a box.

Louise said to go ahead and self-publish the shorter, original version. At the time, NY was open to previously self-published books. Within a month after its release, that changed. Yes. That's how fast things are changing. Still, I finished increasing the word count to 70,000, and Louise started shopping it out.

New York was almost as in love with it as Louise had been. In fact, we got several very pleasant NOs from huge publishers like Penguin, Orbit,

---

1 Direct Message on Twitter

and Simon & Schuster, saying that they loved it, but they couldn't sell the Male 1st person POV.

Remember what I said about the boxes?

In the meantime, the Kindle version of *Avalon Revisited* took off. It hit the top 20 on Amazon's Gothic Romance best seller list, and it remained in the top 40 for over four months.

Why?

Who knows?

I wasn't marketing it, not like I was the Rowan books. I tweeted and blogged and such, but it must have been the mixture of the niche Steampunk marketing, the Paranormal Romance, and the beautiful book cover that helped it reach that status. That, and word-of-mouth.

WOM is gold.

After a three years, *Avalon Revisited*, still sells four times more copies every month than the three Rowan books combined. In fact, it has recently been re-released by an indie press, and there is a sequel, of sorts, called *Avalon Revamped* on the way.

So the Olivia experiment continues. Most of my appearances over the past three years have been as Olivia, as she's far more interesting (elegant and mysterious) with her shiny red hair in her tight corset and fluffy bustle, and that attracts customers.

More customers means more sales.

Marketing Maxim #4: It's a numbers game.

Even though I've recently abandoned the wig and corset for a more down-to-earth, writerly image, the following I created as the Clockwork Coquette as well as the readership from my very personal and dark blog entries, remains. Olivia gave me an outlet for a very dark, painful time in my life, hinted at several times on these pages and explained in detail on Olivia's blog. Through these candid writings, I not only got the catharsis and clarity needed, but I found even more readers. Connected with people on a deep level. Helped people, too.

It's been rather amazing.

Olivia had become a recognizable figure in just a little over a year. Since, she's been the Guest of Honor at several Steampunk Conventions and has won several people's/reader's choice awards. In the end, after all, it's about the writing, not the persona. Olivia certainly does write. Steampunk. Experimental. Literary. Poetry. No boundaries.

Additionally, I have written two dozen short stories and several poems as Olivia, and I've had this fiction and poetry accepted for publication in a variety of anthologies, podcasts, and journals, both on and offline.

Olivia will keep going. She is the persona who has had the most success, so she is the persona that gets the most energy. I'm in the process of morphing everything over to Olivia Grey. Once the *Rowan of the Wood* series is complete with the fifth and final book, *Spirit of the Otherworld*, everything will be published under O. M. Grey.

All in all, O. M. Grey has been a wildly successful experiment, and we can all learn from her. She has a unique image. She doesn't censor herself, so she writes about controversial topics on love, sex, and relationships. She also writes extensively on the darker side of love, covering abusive relationships, sexual assault, and sexual predators.

In fact, that's when her blog stats started going up, by the way.

Way up.

Rule #1 in blogging: connect with readers. Olivia has connected with countless survivors of sexual assault/rape and victims of other human cruelty and abuse.

I suppose one thing we all have in common is having experienced the agony of betrayal. Yep. Solidarity.

So, keep it simple.
Don't censor yourself.
Know the rules, then break them.
Be fearless.
HAVE FUN.

O. M. GREY

PHOTO BY NEITHER NOIR PHOTOGRAPHY

WHERE TO MARKET YOUR BOOK

1. BOOKSTORE SIGNINGS

Picture this: It's your first bookstore signing. You have dreamt about this day since you heard your first author speak and they signed a copy of their book. And here you are, a published author. You've spent months, if not years, writing your masterpiece, and finally it is out there in the hands of your readers.

You show up at Barnes & Noble, ready to sign book after book as customers wait in line to meet you.

You are, after all, a published author.

However, when you get to the bookstore, you see a small poster set in the doorway with your picture and signing time. If you're really lucky Barnes & Noble has put a poster in the window, too. You walk in to meet the CRM, and you find that they've gone home for the evening. You introduce yourself as "the author" and are met with blank stares. One of the employees sets you up at your table, because you're super lucky if they're ready for you when you get there, situated near the front door with about twenty copies of your books. Again, if you're really lucky, they ask you if you'd like a drink from their Starbucks kiosk.

Your watch tells you the signing started fifteen minutes ago, but no one is there. You sip on your free frothy mocha and contemplate the meaninglessness of your existence.

The customers who do come into the story purposely avert their eyes and avoid you and your table of books like they might catch some incurable disease if they even just look at you.

Seriously.

Our first book signing was definitely an eye-opener.

Don't let the above scenario be you. There are things you can do to ensure you have the best book signing that you can as an unknown, emerging author.

We found that the more the CRM (Community Relations Manager) at a Barnes & Noble did to promote our book, the better the book signing, meaning the more books sold. This is really hit or miss. Some CRMs are very serious about their jobs, and those were the best book signings we ever had. Others aren't so concerned. Booking authors is just another task on their long list of things to do.

It came to the point that we knew whether or not it would be a good signing as soon as we walked through those double glass doors. If there was a poster in the window, one in the foyer, and the CRM was actually there (and even greeted us!), then it was a successful signing. And by a successful signing I mean we signed 10-15 books as opposed to the 2-3 if the CRM wasn't there and if there weren't posters in the window.

Again. The key is to be seen.

At our best bookstore signing, we signed over 30 books. In fact, we sold out of Barnes & Nobles' stock and had to go into our personal stash. (Always have books with you, by the way.)

That was certainly a very good day.

Thirty books is incredible for an unknown author at a book signing. What made this signing different from the others?

- It was on a Sunday afternoon. Weekends are always better.
- The CRM had advertised our appearance for an entire two weeks before we arrived.
- She set us up in the middle of the store, right across from Starbucks and in front of the Children's section. This worked extremely well for that store because it had two entrances (normally it's best to be by the entrance).
- The CRM had also sent out a press release to the local paper, so our appearance was listed in there.

If only all book signings could all be that way. That was, unfortunately, the exception, certainly not the rule. Most bookstore signings we signed fewer than 10 books. That's the nature of life as an unknown author. You are doing the equivalent of "pounding the pavement" to reach your readers. One. At. A. Time.

TIPS FOR BOOKSTORE SIGNINGS

- When scheduling an author appearance at a bookstore, **talk with the marketing and community outreach person**. At Barnes & Noble, this position is called the Community Relations Manager (CRM). The email address for the CRM is always: crm####@ bn.com. The #### is replaced by the four-digit store number, which can be found at the end of the URL for that particular store from the http://www.barnesandnoble.com website. Click on "Stores & Events" in the top menu and search for stores. Here is where your event should be listed as well. It doesn't hurt to drop that into the conversation with the CRM. "Will our event be listed on the B&N Website?" ...with the appropriate excitement in your voice.

- **Advertising.** Always. If people don't know about the event, then how could they possibly come? Ask that the CRM to put it on the website, in their newsletter, and to send a press release to the local paper. Ask them what they normally do for author signings, and tell them that you've had the greatest success when there is a window and in-store display for at least a week ahead of time.

- **Dress up.** Look good. Yes, you are an author, an artist. Your work is what matters, not your appearance. But remember you are going to be in the public eye, and no one knows who you are yet. Whereas I advise to dress in costume at places like fantasy conventions and the like, the bookstore is no place for this. If you are dressed in costume, customers will be a little freaked out. You will have enough trouble catching their eye. Steampunk seems to be the exception to this. The finery of a Steampunk Victorian outfit catches the eye whether you are at a fantasy convention, bookstore signing, or restaurant. People respond to elegance.

- **Be assertive, but not aggressive.** As mentioned, most are going to avert their eyes. Those people who are obviously trying to avoid you, let them be. They don't want to be sold to and probably came to the bookstore to get one specific thing. However, there are those who will look over at you and your table out of curiosity. If they look for more than one second, introduce yourself. Hand them a card. Pitch your book.

- Some CRMs schedule months in advance, so query early.
- You'll encounter **four types of people at book signings**, listed in descending order of frequency:
  1. Those who seriously avert their eyes. They don't want to be bothered.
  2. Those who curiously look at you and your table.
  3. Those who come up to your table enthusiastically to hear about your book.
  4. Those who come up for publishing/writing advice and stay there talking to you for thirty minutes or more. Oh yes they do. Be polite, but don't hesitate to say "Excuse me" when a potential customer comes into view.

2. SOCIAL NETWORKING

FACEBOOK

Some experts say that Facebook is definitely the way to go for marketing, as less than 10% of adult Americans use Twitter, according to eMarketer.com.[1] Whereas Facebook will reach over half of all internet users.

That said, Facebook is mostly used to make personal connections, not for marketing your wares. Facebook users get annoyed very quickly if you're continually selling to them. Well, Twitter users do, too. Come to think of it, everyone gets pretty annoyed at that.

Definitely create a profile page for your more personal updates. This is a great place to reconnect with old friends and family, as well as build a fan base. But you will want most of your readers and "fans" to "like" a "fan page," rather than friend you on Facebook. It keeps things a little separate, but you will end up using your profile for both.

---

1 "Facebook Reaches Majority of Web Users." eMarketer. 24 February 2011. Web. 04 Apr. 2011.

Create a "fan page," where readers and fans can "like" your content. Whereas you can only have up to 5,000 "friends," you can have unlimited "fans!"

Follow how to do this step-by-step below. This is different than it was in the first edition. Facebook has changed about six times in the past two years, so if these instructions no longer work, just Google "How to create a Facebook page" and you will find lots of instructions.

HOW TO CREATE A FACEBOOK FAN PAGE

1. Go to https://www.facebook.com/pages/create.php, or at the bottom of any Facebook window, follow the link that says "Create a Page." But be quick! It will try to load more status updates forever and ever.

2. Choose *Artist, band or public figure*. Choose the category *Author* and put in your name or pen name. Agree to the terms and conditions and *Get started*.

3. Put in a nice author picture, preferably the same one you will use on Twitter and Goodreads, et al., as you'll want to create a recognizable "brand." Put in an eye-catching "cover image" as well. This is the large banner-type image behind your author photo. Use something inspirational, more pictures of you, or even a picture of your book. People like looking at pictures. It's the first thing they'll see, so make it a good one. Go into Photoshop and create an image specifically for this purpose: 851px wide x 315px tall.

4. Explore the *edit page* choices and see how you can best promote your new page to your current email list, Facebook friends, and more. Be sure to fill out the BIO section (remember when I had you write those earlier?) under *Basic Information* and add some pictures. People like looking at pictures. Have I mentioned?

5. Choose the option to connect this with your Twitter account under *Resources*, but don't link Twitter to Facebook. Clarification: let Facebook posts go to Twitter, but don't let your Twitter feed

post to Facebook. Twitter is a different, more loquacious animal. Facebook users cannot handle such frequent updates. There is no faster way to lose your Facebook friends or to be hidden from their view.

Through Facebook, one can create events and invite friends or fan page followers. This is especially helpful if you target your marketing geographically. Contests don't work. Facebook ads don't work. Seriously. Don't waste your money. Keep your apps and games and other such things to a minimum. You want your Facebook page to be clean[1].

The most important thing with Facebook as with any social networking is to participate in the community. Read the news feed. "Like" other people's posts and comments. Comment on status updates. Post pictures and share your life. People want to know who you are. You can give as much or as little of yourself on Facebook as you'd like. But if you plan to keep it mostly professional, you will still need to post pictures of your book signings and events and tweet ups and such.

After you've created your page, you will be able to use Facebook as your profile or as your page. Toggle back and forth in the settings drop-down menu on the top right (looks like a little cog).

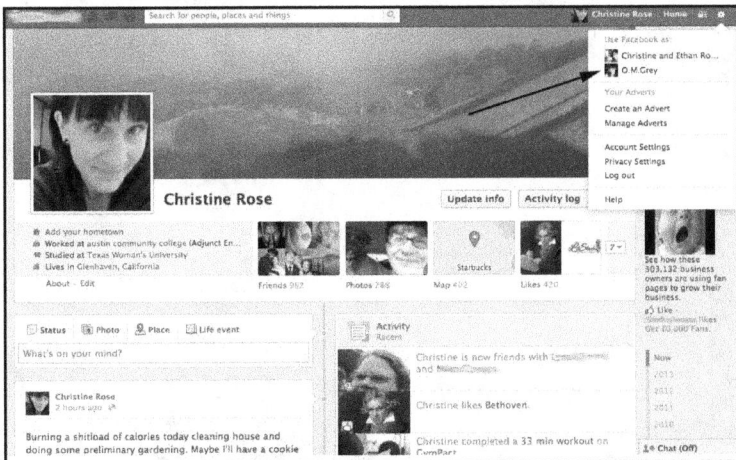

---

1 "Why Most Facebook Marketing Doesn't Work." ReadWriteWeb. 17 Feb. 2011. Web. 02 Apr. 2011.

On a Facebook page, as administrator, you will be able to see the Admin Panel. If you can't, click on **Show** near the top right, and it will pull it down for you. This is your dashboard. From your Admin Panel, you can see Insights, Messages (to your page as opposed to your profile), new likes, and notifications (who liked or commented on what status).

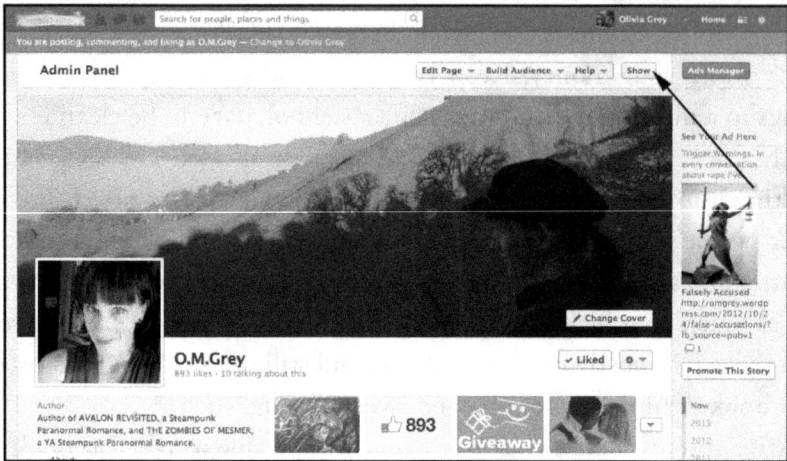

Facebook page with Admin Panel hidden

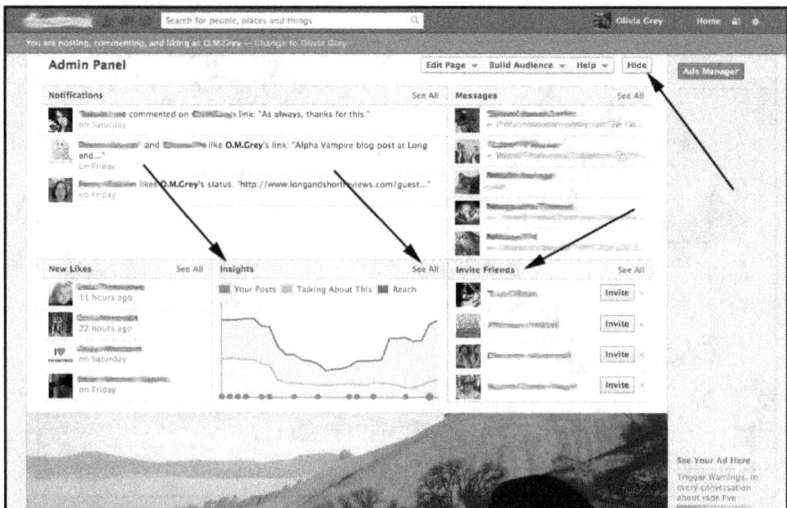

Facebook page with Admin Panel shown.
Also note *Insights, See All,* and *Invite Friends.*

You can also Invite Friends. Do this. Right now. Click on as many **Invite** buttons as Facebook will let you. Then come back tomorrow and do that again. These are inviting your friends from your personal profile to "like" your fan page. Those who do will want professional updates as well as personal ones.

The **Insights** section is important. You can expand this, as well as any Admin section, by clicking the "Seel All" link in the top right corner of the particular section. The Insights show your statistics. How many posts. How many likes. How many people are talking about this page. How many people you reach, etc.

It even breaks it down into demographics and location! Under "Talking about this," you can find how many males compared to females are talking about your page. How old they are. Where they live. Etc.

It's very useful for analyzing your marketing efforts. Explore this thoroughly for the best Facebook marketing results.

JOIN OR CREATE A FACEBOOK GROUP

Since the first edition of this book, Facebook has rejuvenated their groups. Groups are a great way to have themed discussions or to get a community of people with similar interests together.

You can make a Facebook Group for your book, but I would advise against that at this point. No one knows you yet, and they certainly don't know your book. It will end up being just one more thing to update. Once you've built a few thousand followers who are actively discussing your inspired prose and intricate plot twists, THEN start a group. In fact, by then one of your fans will likely have done it for you.

Still, joining other groups can be great. But be forewarned! Don't join a group to post links to your books every day. People will hide you and ignore you. Join a group to interact with the community. To be yourself. To contibute to a larger conversation or debate.

Once they all know and love you, THEN post one or two links to your work. No more, and only when something is newly released.

Alternatively, post links to your blog, because you'll be blogging about relevant topics. Right?

Post links to things that they will find interesting. Post links to things that will help them. If those links are on your blog, all the better, because your blog will have links to buy your books! Hub. Remember?

Using this thinking, you can create your own Facebook Group, not around your book, but around a topic that will be of interest to you and your target demographic.

Say your book is a mystery with emphasis on the darker side or even foresnic medicine. Create or join a Facebook group that discusses forensics or serial killers or BONES, the TV show. People who like those things will automatically be interested in your mystery book WHEN they get to know and like YOU first.

Participating in a group is a great way to do this.

CREATE FACEBOOK EVENTS

I don't know about you, but I'm about sick to death of being invited to a gazillion Facebook Events.

Still, they work.

That's why there are so many.

Groups can be used for anything from a book signing to a book or story release to a blog tour or contest (total waste of time, contests), create a Facebook event and invite ALL YOUR FRIENDS.

That's right. ALL OF THEM!

Now this is a real pain because Facebook only lets you choose one at a time, so you have to go through all your friends, clicking each one. Unless...you Google "how to mass invite your friends on Facebook event" and follow the directions you find. It's always changing, so I won't even bother putting a specific link here. This will save you so much time.

Most won't reply, just as I don't reply to most of the Events I get, but some will. It's another way to be seen.

Again, you can't do this every week, or you'll be annoying. Do it around special releases or events, and it will work well for you.

Once an event is created, you can post status updates in the Event itself. Notifications for those updates will be sent to those who said they'd attend your event.

Events don't have to be physical; they can be virtual (online).

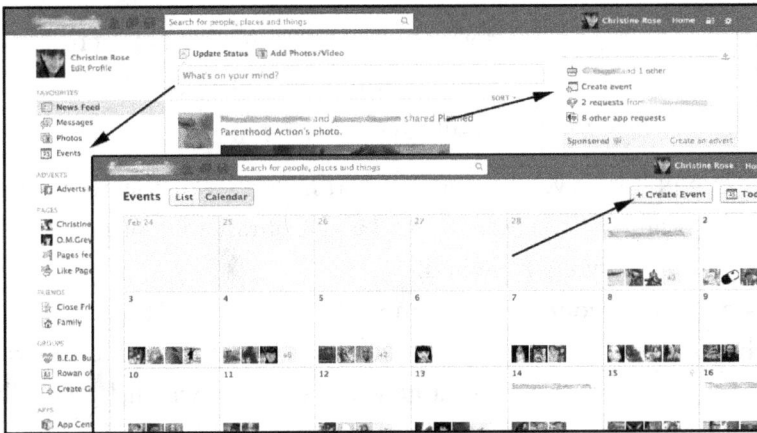

Follow these steps to create a Facebook Event:

1. Click on the Facebook logo on the top left of the window
2. Choose **Events** from the left sidebar (or **Create event** on right)
3. Near the top left, click on **+ Create Event**
4. In the window that pops up, name your event, give it an interesting description, choose your privacy options (I suggest **Public**) and place. Leave the place blank or put in a website unless it's an actual physical event.
5. After you save that information, the next thing to do is add a picture. People like looking at pictures. Click on the space for the image near the top left and choose **Add Event Photo**.
6. Then, **Invite Friends** from the button near the top left. This will open a window with all your friends. Normally, you would have to click each and every one which could take hours if you have a lot of friends, Fortunately, we have Google, as I mentioned above. This is where you use that fancy formula to invite every-

one at once. Scroll down to the bottom of the "Invite Friends" window. Keep scrolling until all your friends are loaded. Then put in the javascript code from your Google search in the URL bar at the top of your browser window.

7.   Wait while the javascript code works its magic. I used the following, but it's best to find it online and just copy/paste.

```
javascript:elms=document.getElementsByName("ch
eckableitems[]");for(i=0;i<elms.length;i++){if (elms[i].
type="checkbox" )elms[i].click()};
```

It will take several seconds if you have a lot of friends. You may be prompted to enter a CAPTCHA phrase to continue.

8.   Voila! Everyone is invited!

I did this for a contest (Yes. I know. I go on and on about how pointless they are, and they are. More about this under the contest section.) for a simple PDF giveaway of a new anthology in which I had a short story. Within two minutes of posting the event, I had people commenting on the blog post that had been up for two days without a single comment.

Facebook Events work. So does direct marketing by asking for a specific, easy action. More on that soon.

You can do this either through your profile or by using Facebook as your fan page; however, if you do it under your fan page, you must share it on your fan page wall and followers will have to "join" themselves. You can't invite friends since you don't have "friends" as a fan page, you have fans or followers.

FACEBOOK EVENTS TIP

Use your Facebook profile to join an event created by your Facebook fan page, then invite your friends.

PROMOTION & AUTOMATION TIPS

Utilize the "Social Plugins" section of your Facebook fan page by putting a "Like Button" or "Follow Button" on your blog. To do this, go to *Edit Page* from your Facebook fan page. Click on *Update Info* choice in the drop-down menu and then on *Resources* on the left sidebar. Under *Connect with People* click on *Use Social Plugins* to see all your choices. Choose *Follow Button*, which will lead you to a page to copy an HTML code. You will likely need to paste the HTML code generated there into a "text" block (found under *Widgets* from your Dashboard in WordPress, see below) in a widget enabled WordPress/Blogger theme, or get your web designer to put it on your traditional website.

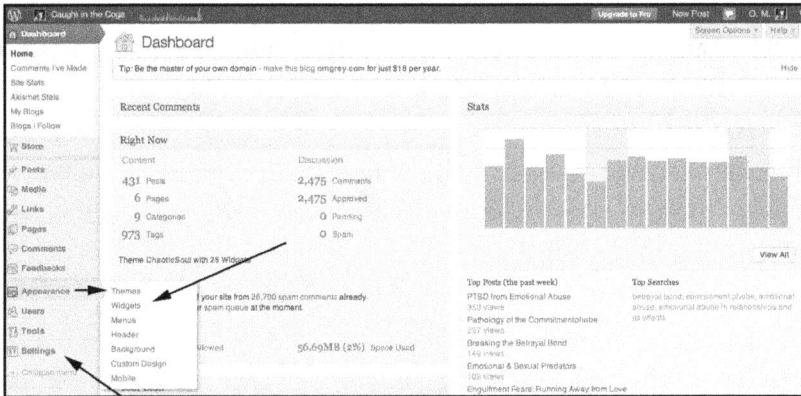

Link your blog to Facebook, so whenever you have a new post, it automatically posts on your Facebook page. This is especially easy with a WordPress blog. From your WordPress Dashboard, scroll down until you see the *Settings* heading on the left (see above). Choose *Sharing*, and there you can add Facebook, Twitter, and more. I often get more blog visitors coming from my Facebook fan page, which currently only has under 900 fans, than I get from my Twitter feed which has over ten thousand followers.

Go figure.

Under the *Basic Information* link from the *Edit Page->Update Info* selection on your Facebook page Admin Panel, you can select a username for your page. This is important because you want to direct people to your Facebook page without having a long, complicated URL. Choose your name,[1] if its available. For example, the fan page for O. M. Grey looks like this: http://www.facebook.com/omgrey

Easy to remember. Easy to find.

Group your Top Fans and interact with them regularly by utilizing the list building option in Facebook. As you progress, you will find that there are certain people who really like you and your work. They're the ones who comment on your blog and on your status updates. Even the ones who consistently "like" your updates. Group them all together in one list so that you can pay special attention to them, nurturing that precious connection.

From any of one of your "top fan's" posts or comments, hover over their name and a small window will pop up. From there, hover over the "friends" tab in that pop-up window. Click on "Add to another list" then create the "Top Fans" list or add to it after it's been created. This list, as well as your other lists like Close Friends, Family, and more, will show up in your left sidebar, accessible everytime you click on the Facebook logo in the top left.

Have fun on Facebook. It's a great tool, and you must learn how to effectively use this tool for your book and marketing plan. Remember not to just talk about yourself and your book, you must interact with the community. This, as in all social marketing, can become quite time consuming, so set aside ten or twenty minutes in the morning while you have your coffee to socialize on Facebook, then perhaps take two or three breaks a day for five-ten minutes each. More than that and you can get sucked in. The key is little snippets and interactions periodically throughout your work day.

---

1 Brand your name, not your book title.

TWITTER

Twitter can be another powerful marketing tool, some say far more powerful than Facebook. I think they work best together. These two, as well as all social networking tools, are meant to drive traffic to your blog. Your blog is the hub.

I've known authors who have sold hundreds of books just through Twitter, but one must know the most beneficial way to use Twitter. It is, after all, just a tool. It will not sell books for you.

In 2009, I had the honor of being one of the top 100 Twitter Authors as determined by Mashable.com. I was right up there with Neil Gaiman (@neilhimself) and Meg Cabot (@megcabot), among others.

Twitter is like being at a huge, diverse party. There are millions of conversations going on all at once, all in 140-character snippets. Your task is to find the group who is talking about and interested in reading and the types of books you write. Find other authors or industry professionals. After all, I have a New York agent because she found me on Twitter. I've connected with countless authors at all success levels because of Twitter and have established some close friendships because of Twitter. It is a wonderful way to connect with agents, editors, other authors, and potential readers. This is where you get to know them and they get to know you around the central cyberspace water cooler. It is a powerful tool if you learn how to use it.

Utilizing Twitter for marketing your book, or any product, is four-fold:

1. **Marketing/Industry Tweets.** This is where you talk about your book and where to get it. This is where you quote a review of your book and link back to the review site. This is where you promote other people's books (Cross-Promotion is GOLD). In every tweet where you mention your book, add a link (preferably an Amazon Associate link, to be covered in the Amazon section) so that whether they buy your book or something else, you get a few pennies for the sale. These tweets can also be about the publishing industry or your specific topic. Under @omgrey, for example, I tweet many things having to do with #Steampunk, as

that's the subgenre in which "O. M. Grey" writes. And...it's all automated. I'll get to automation shortly.

2. **ReTweets (RT).** When you RT someone, they see you. They see that what they say is important to you or interesting enough that you want to share it with your followers as well. You want to RT, and you want to be RTed. RT things that catch your interest. Things that are funny. Things that are informative or inspirational. When someone RTs you, send them an @Reply thanking them for doing so. Twittiquette.

3. **Personal Tweets.** These are tweets about that mocha you love so much or what you're doing. Walking in the rain. Craving that first cup of coffee. Trying to type with your cat on the keyboard. Twitter is a community, and your followers will want to get to know you. They do this by reading your personal tweets and your personal interactions. Another great thing to tweet are inspirational or funny quotes. Be yourself. If you don't have the gift of wit, then tweet to your strengths.

4. **@Replies, aka Mentions or @Tags**, or personal interaction. To get people to interact with you, you must first interact with them. An @Reply is when you reply to a specific tweeter, thereby carrying on a conversation with them. The more you @Reply, the more you build a community on Twitter. When you @Reply someone, it shows up in both your Twitter feed as well in the recipients "mentions" feed. DMs (Direct Messages) are a more private was to communicate for things that shouldn't be public, like email addresses, phone numbers, etc. Alternatively, it doesn't have to be a reply, which is why they're now called "Mentions." If you want another Tweeter to see your tweet, you @tag them.

It is a healthy mixture of these four things that will give you the greatest success on Twitter. Before you do any of this wild tweeting, however, you will need to create a Twitter account. Your twitter name should be your author name or your pen name. Whatever name you want people to remember[1].

---

1 Have I mentioned? Brand. Your. Name.

HOW TO SIGN UP FOR TWITTER

1. Go to Twitter.com
2. Click on "Sign Up"
3. Enter your full name, a username (again this should be your name or your pen name, alternatively it could be your book, but you will eventually have more than one book, so it's best to stick with your name. **Your brand is your name.**), a password, and a valid email address. (Tip: There are so many Twitter cons and hackers, choose a good, strong password.)
4. Click "Create my account."

Once you have your Twitter account, the next step is to personalize your profile then start building your follower base, otherwise you are shouting in to the darkness.

PERSONALIZE YOUR TWITTER PROFILE

On the top right corner of the Twitter browser window, click on the cog. An image of a cog usually indicates settings, whether on Facebook, Twitter, or your iPhone. There should be a down-pointing arrow next to the cog indicating a drop-down menu. Choose *Settings*.

The first choice on the left menu is *Account*. Ensure that *Protect My Tweets* is not checked. You don't want your tweets protected, otherwise no one other than your followers can see your tweets.

Whether or not you *Add a location to your tweets* is up to you. If you choose this option, every tweet you send can have GPS coordinations of where you are. This can be fun if you are at a party or a book signing, but it can also be potentially dangerous. I have had fans show up at a coffee shop from where I checked-in on Facebook. When it's public, it's public. But here on Twitter, when you're tweeting from the web (I'll go into tweeting from other programs and from your phone shortly), you can choose just how specific you want your location to appear from exact location, neighborhood, or town. You also have the choice to keep your location off any specific tweet. Turning the "Add a location to your tweets" gives you the option before every tweet.

The third item on the menu is **Mobile**. This is to set up your mobile phone to tweet via text message. If you want to tweet on-the-go, something I highly recommend, and you do not have a smart phone, this is a good option to set up. If you do have a smart phone, like an iPhone, Blackberry, etc., then there are better ways to tweet on-the-go, like through the free Twitter App.

Under **Email notifications** you can choose how often, if ever, Twitter contacts you via email. Set your own preferences here. Same goes for **Design**. Choose whatever background you like the best, alter colors, or even upload a personalized background that contains your book cover and other pertinent information.

The **Profile** menu option is very important. Here you will upload a picture of yourself, or some sort of icon to represent you, as well as a header. This header is much like the Facebook cover image. Your profile icon can be your latest book cover, your dog, or anything, really. I suggest putting up a picture of yourself, and one that is a good likeness[1]. You want your future fans to recognize you when you have a "tweet up" (meeting your twitter followers). Put your author name next to "Name" and your city in **Location**, unless you want to be clever or mysterious. For the header, choose something interesting. This can be your book cover/s or you at a book signing, or just something inspirational or dark and mysterious, whatever tone will fit you and your work.

This next step is very important. Under **Website** in your profile set up, put in your blog or author website, even if this is just a Facebook page. Put something here. This is how your future followers will find out more about you and your book.

Under **Bio**, write a short bio of who you are and mention your book or at least that you are an author. Again, be clever. Remember all those Bios I had you write before? Copy/Paste. So easy.

---

1 To maximize branding, use the same picture on Twitter, Facebook, Goodreads, etc.

Now that your profile is all set up, it's time to build your follower base. The best way to gain followers is to follow others and begin interacting with them by RTing their tweets and @Replying to them.

A FEW WORDS ABOUT HASHTAGS (#)

Hashtags, which look like this: #, enable you to follow specific topics on Twitter. By adding a hashtag to your tweets, you can join in on larger conversations. This method reaches more people than one can by simply @replying. Popular hashtags for writers are the #amwriting tag, #selfpublishing tag, and the fun #1k1hr tag, which is a place to join other authors getting in the zone to write at least one thousand (1K) words and for at least one hour (1HR) before stopping.

Wednesdays are Writer Wednesdays, or #WW. Here you can find many other authors on Twitter with whom to interact.

Fridays are Follow Friday, or #FF. Again, great place to find new people.

If you've ever heard someone talk about "trending topics" on Twitter, this is when there are millions of people using the same key words or hashtags. You can look at trending topics and join in those larger conversations as well, or just watch the TwitterVerse stream by.

Following trends and using hashtags is also a wonderful way to find quality followers. Follow them first, interact with them by using @ replies, and hopefully they'll follow you back.

By following these discussions, you can tap into a larger Twitter community that falls into your niche, meet new friends, and learn a lot about social networking, the business of publishing, and what you're up against as an emerging author.

Popular Hashtags (#) for Writers
#yalitchat #steampunkchat #selfpublishing
#amwriting #1k1hr #writechat #writersroad
#litchat #kitlitchat #publishing
#WW #WriterWednesday #authors

AUTOMATING TWEETS & OTHER RESOURCES

As you become Twitter savvy, especially if you use a program like TweetDeck to follow different threads or TweetAdder for automation, you can schedule a lot of these tweets ahead of time, or even schedule them to tweet periodically through the day whether or not you're actually on Twitter. This is essential for marketing, as you cannot spend twelve hours a day on Twitter and actually get any writing done.

Trust me.

It's very easy to spend twelve hours a day on Twitter.

TweetDeck will auto-shorten URLs, which helps since you only have 140 characters to say what you want to say. TweetAdder will do the same, plus it will space out your automated tweets an intervals you choose.

Scheduling tweets is especially useful for recurring tweets. These are tweets about your book, someone else's book,[1] your Facebook fan page, and marketing tweets, the first of the four-fold Twitter strategy. TweetAdder is perfect for this, but it is not free. There are other free services online, but more maintenance is required.

With **TweetAdder**, you set up those recurring tweets once, leave it running, set how often you want the program to auto-tweet (I suggest at least an hour or two between tweets, and only between 8:00 am and 8:00 pm), and walk away. This program will take care of all your marketing tweets, so now you can focus on RTs, @Replies, and personal tweets.

Something I started doing last year was scheduling recurring tweets that linked back to old blog posts. Every 1 to 2 hours, another tweet goes live, either linking to one of my stories, my books using my Amazon Associate link, or one of my many past blog posts, podcasts, or reviews. I have found this invaluable! It has brought so many more readers to my blog. The nature of blogs are to have new, fresh content often, but that leaves a lot of great things you've written deep in the archives.

---

1 Cross-promotion is GOLD.

Do this: create a simple list on Notepad (PC) or TextEdit (Mac) where each new line contains a new tweet. Save it to your desktop. You can then upload that .txt file directly into TweetAdder, setting to post each in a random order at an interval of your choosing. Again, I recommend one every hour or two. In between those marketing tweets, you will be RTing, mention others through the @tag, and tweeting personal stuff.

This is what the first few lines of my .txt file looks like for the O. M. Grey automated tweets:

Post: "Of Grace & Gratitude" http://goo.gl/0QTnd - Examples of effective and ineffective communication

Post: "O. M. Grey on GetLusty for Couples" #Podcast http://goo.gl/t5ndV

Post: "Opening Up to Intimacy" - how to build intimacy with your partner http://goo.gl/hUIaJ

Post: "Out, Damned Spot, Out" - http://goo.gl/LaV8d - Outing rapists when the law fails survivors

Post: "Overcoming Shame" - letting go of the shame of your betrayer and redefining yourself. http://goo.gl/qJaDR

Post: "Pathological Passion" - stemming from the Greek pathos, meaning "to suffer" Hmmmmm. http://goo.gl/Zbeu3

Post: "Pathology of the Commitmentphobe" - a serious psychological phobia. Take note & take care. http://goo.gl/njYzd

Post: "People Who Hide Behind 'Poly'" - http://goo.gl/XoGaQ #polyamory

These continue on through all my blog posts, poems, podcasts, short fiction, and reviews. Each starting on their own line. It takes over a week for them to all post on Twitter via automation. It's great because it's not too repetitive, and I still get people seeing something I wrote two years ago for the first time! It's brilliant, really. I wish I could say it was my idea.

TweetAdder is worth the money, and then some.

If you prefer not to buy something now, you can use a service like FutureTweet or the desktop client TweetDeck, which has a schedule option, but you must take the time each morning to schedule marketing tweets throughout that day.

In TweetDeck, which I highly recommend in addtion to TweetAdder, you can see several feeds at once, like your main feed, mentions, DMs. Additionally, you can customize columns to follow certain hashtags or keywords. You can even make special list columns where you siphon out certain followers to interact with more regularly or to promote. If you use TweetDeck to for your promotional tweets, just set aside ten to twenty minutes a day and schedule your tweets periodically throughout that day.

Although TweetDeck is brilliant for organizing feeds and scheduling tweets over the course of the day, it will not automatically find people and follow them. You can purchase programs to build your follower base and bulk follows hundreds a day by focusing on key words. The program I used was TweetAdder, and I cannot recommend it enough. It's not only great for building a follower base but also for scheduling recurring tweets and other automated services. As I mentioned, TweetAdder is not free, but it is well worth the money to save you time. After all, marketing, although extremely important, is not the only thing you have to do with your day. You do want to have time to write.

Also a free online resource called Tweepi looks quite promising[1].

The biggest problem with using an automated program to build your follower base is that it's not perfect. It will search tweets and/or profiles with a given keyword(s) and follow them. A portion of these will follow you back. Then the program, after a certain amount of days, will unfollow anyone who didn't follow you. You will get many followers in a short amount of time, but they will not necessarily be *quality followers*, meaning they will unlikely be interested in or interact with you the way you hope[2]. It's much better, albeit very slow, to build your following

---

1 http://tweepi.com
2 Because of this, I no longer use TweetAdder to build followers. I just use it for the automated tweets.

organically. Still, automated programs do have their benefits. After all, marketing is a numbers game.

Keep in mind that Twitter has become overrun with spammers, people just trying to sell things, and the Twitter community has long since grown weary of this.

Don't be a spammer.

Yes, you wrote a book.

Yes, it's great.

But from the perspective of your thousands of potential followers, they say "sure, you and everyone else on here."

Remember, you are a grain of sand on a long stretch of beach. You want people to see you, to have a reason to look. Not to have a reason to pass you by and dismiss you. Content. Connect. Cross-promote.

Please don't spam[3]

HOW AUTOMATING TWITTER SAVED MY CAREER

Okay. That might be a bit of an overstatement, but it caught your attention! As I mentioned before, I set up .txt documents with links to all my blog posts, podcasts, book links, reviews, and more, then uploaded those .txt files to TweetAdder to randomly post throughout the day and week.

2011 and 2012 were extremely difficult years for me, personally, which you can read all about on http://omgrey.wordpress.com if you're interested, and there were times I could hardly function in life, let alone writing, social networking, marketing, blogging, and the like. It's when I wrote so many short stories because I couldn't focus on something as long as a novel. I also wrote a lot of blog posts under O. M. Grey, as I could talk about what was happening with me there.

On http://christinerose.wordpress.com, I couldn't talk about those things for a variety of reasons. Again, mostly personal. So my blog Of Marketing, Mochas, and Mayhem at http://christinerose.wordpress. com was rather neglected.

---

3 SPAM means talking just about your book and sending specific messages telling people where to buy it.

I fell way behind on the publishing industry and marketing trends. I wasn't reading or reviewing books anymore, so I wasn't promoting other authors as I wanted to.

I was surviving, and it took most of my energy, mental and physical, to do just that.

You can see through my archives just how sparse those years were in blogging. I started podcasting fiction because I could get it together enough to record audio for a few hours, but rarely to write anything new.

This is how TweetAdder and automated tweets saved my career. As I only had to remember to upload those tweets once a week or so to TweetAdder, @christinerose had *something* being posted to it. Granted, I wasn't marketing using my 4-fold Twitter approach, so it wasn't as effective as it could've been, but it was something rather than just disappearing for two years. Through these automated tweets, I found new readers. I found loyal fans and followers. I found that I was still being recommended for #FF and #WW because of the work I had done in the past. Because of TweetAdder, I didn't fall down the memory hole.

Thanks to the first edition of this book, my *Rowan of the Wood* fantasy series, and the work I did on my blog and podcasts around Publishing & Marketing Realities, automated tweets kept finding me new readers even when I was unable to produce new content.

Brilliant.

Yes, highly recommend TweetAdder and automated tweets.

Market yourself. Market your blog. Market your books.

NICHE MARKETING TIP

If you can find a tight niche for your work or a specific hashtag that works for you, there is a wonderful way to tweet a relevant topic and have it all automated. Under @omgrey, I tweet about many things #Steampunk, and it's all automated. To do this, I utilize two services: **Google Alerts and TwitterFeed.**

GOOGLE ALERTS

First set up a Google Alert feed. To do this, you will need a Google account. You can use the same one as your Gmail account if you have one. If not, it's a good idea to create one, as Google has many wonderful resources.

- At Google.com, click on the *more* link on the top menu, then click on *even more* in that drop down menu.
- Scroll down until you see a little gold bell with the word *Alerts* next to it under *Specialized Searches*. Click on that.
- This next page is where you will set your search terms. In my case, for O. M. Grey, I chose "Steampunk." This is a tight enough niche that it's not overrun. You can also use "vampire" or "romance" or "publishing" or "self-publishing" or whatever else describes the niche you'd like to be discussing on Twitter. The tighter the niche, however, the more effective this will be.
- From the drop down menus beneath the *Search terms* box, choose:
  - Type: Everything
  - How often: As-it-happens
  - Volume: Everything
- Put your email in and click on *Create Alert.*
- After you verify your email, go back to your Google Alert page. You don't want all those alerts cluttering up your inbox. Change the *Deliver to* from "email" to "feed." (You can also create another alert with your name and/or book title in it and have that delivered to your email box. It's an interesting way to keep up with people talking about you or your book.)
- Click *save*, then click on the word *feed*. Copy the URL in the top box. You will need this for the next step. There probably won't be anything in the feed for several hours, so wait until items are showing up in the feed before proceeding to step two.
- Side note: Set up a Google Alert with your name and your book title. Have those emailed to you daily. Then you'll know when someone is talking about you or your book.

TIP: If you don't know terms like "feed" or "RSS" or anything else on these pages, or my explanations aren't sufficient for your understanding, Google it. Seriously. Google is your best friend, along with Amazon.

TWITTER FEED

- Go to TwitterFeed.com and log in (set up an account or use your OpenID)
- Click on *Create New Feed*
- Give a name for your feed and then paste that URL you just copied into the feed box.
- Under *Advanced Settings,* choose how you would like your content to be published (remember 140 character limit on Twitter). Be sure to put in a hashtag under *Post Suffix*, like #Steampunk PlsRT. So every post will have the hashtag and a RT request. Automatically.
- Check for new posts (choose 1-3 hours) and post up to (pick only 1-3, because you don't want to be a spammer). I only post one every three hours, but you can post more than that if you'd like. One an hour would be fine.
- Click *Continue* at the bottom. On this next page, click on "Twitter" and put in your Twitter information.
- You're done. Automated, relevant Tweets.

TWITTER TIPS
DON'Ts:
- Spam. I know I've already said that, but it's important enough to say it again.
- Don't send auto Direct Messages to your new followers advertising your book. This is extremely annoying. And it's SPAM.
- Don't send random @Replies advertising your book. This really irks me, and I will block and report spam on anyone who does this. And it's SPAM.

DOs:

- Be helpful. The best way to gain followers is to help other people promote their books and to help other writers find pertinent industry information.
- Be funny or witty, if you can. People love to be entertained. Most people are on Twitter during their day job, and they are just looking for anything to help the day pass by more quickly. If you can't be funny, RT other humorous tweets. Find funny quotes and tweet those.
- Be inspirational. Sometimes inspirational quotes get the most RTs. Funny quotes, even more.
- Be personable and friendly.
- Talk about something other than yourself and your book.

WHO TO FOLLOW

These authors and other industry professionals are doing it well. Use them and interact with them to start your Twitter community[1].

@Patrick_Alan, @LeannaRenee, @dirtywhitecandy, @KMWeiland, @lizdarvill, @LittleAnimation, @a_crezo (freelance editor), @Bob_Mayer, @JoLynneValerie, @MermaidHel (freelance editor), @KwanaWrites, @KL_Grady, @RachelBrooks07, @paul_e_cooley (author & podcaster), @teemorris (author & podcaster), @kristenlambtx (social networking expert), @teetate (freelance editor), @catarionna (cover artist), @keyboardhussy, @mattdelman, @selfpubreview

In addition to these, find the top twenty journalists/book reviewers on Twitter. Follow them. Interact with them. DO NOT pitch your book to them. Just get to know them and let them get to know you.

YOUTUBE & BOOK TRAILERS

YouTube is another great way to get you and your book out there. Again, especially if you have the gift of humor. Vlogging, video blogging, has become quite popular, and several authors have become bestselling authors because of their vlogging. John Green is one of the most

---

1 @username is how a Twitter username is written. To find them on Twitter, put the username without the @ after http://twitter.com; e.g., http://twitter.com/username

famous authors-turned-best-seller because of YouTube. He and his brother Hank did "Brotherhood 2.0" a few years back, and they gained tens of thousands of followers. They are both very funny and charming, so it worked for them. They are both now quite financially set just from their YouTube activity! In fact, they just performed to a sold-out audience at Carnegie Hall[1].

Making videos is easier than ever. On many phones you can record video and upload it straight to YouTube; however, this isn't the best way as the quality is very low. You will have to learn how to edit video, which is very time consuming, but if you enjoy it, it can do wonders for you. I recommend the book *YouTube: An Insider's Guide to Climbing the Charts*.

Vlogging is a commitment, and it takes several hours a week to keep it up. That's even editing simple videos. For the first year of our promotion, I vlogged twice a week under TheTuberRose, chronicling our travels in the Geekalicious Gypsy Caravan. It was fun, for awhile. Ultimately, I got too few views to keep it up. Like anything in this business, it does take a while to build a following. And YouTube is a social networking platform, too. If you want people to watch your videos, you have to watch theirs. If you already watch a lot of YouTube videos, incoporate it into your marketing strategy.

You can also use YouTube to host your book trailer. A book trailer is like a movie trailer for your book. Again, unless you have decent equipment and a talent for editing video, you will have to hire someone to produce, shoot, and cut your book trailer. However, a book trailer doesn't have to have actors, it can just consist of images and words and music. Spend some time on YouTube and watch some book trailers on there. See which ones work for you and which do not.

Another cool way to utilize YouTube is to read your short stories or poetry on video. This can be very simple or fancily edited. Up to you. Do one of these every so often, then post it in your blog and on your networks. You'll reach a new audience this way.

People like to look at pictures.

---

1 Kaufman, Leslie. "A Novelist and His Brother Sell Out Carnegie Hall." *New York Times*. 16 Jan 2013. Web. 21 March 2013.

GOODREADS, LIBRARYTHING, NING, & MORE

Author sites and other social networks like Goodreads[2], LibraryThing, Steampunk Empire, Ning Groups, etc, can be a great resource. There are far too many to list them all. Although I keep profiles on several, I only have time to update a few. I use Goodreads more than LibraryThing, but I know plenty of authors who prefer LibraryThing.

Goodreads can be linked directly to Facebook and Twitter, as well as the RSS feed to your blog. There is also an iPhone app for it.

I love automation. It saves me so much time.

Now when I review a book on Goodreads, it automatically announces it on my Facebook and Twitter feeds. I also have my blog linked directly into Goodreads, so whenever I publish a new blog post, it populates my Goodreads page, as well as Facebook, Twitter, Tumblr, and LinkedI.

Automation Rocks!

At the very least, create a profile on a few of these sites. If they speak to you, and you like their interface, use them often. If they don't, then set up a reminder once a month to go update your profiles, check your messages, etc.

Like all social networks, you really have to become part of the community, interacting and contributing often, for it to work for you as a marketing tool. Again, focus on two or three, and work those. Keep profiles on the others and update now and again, but really work those two or three networks. Spend time building your friends lists and connections, interacting with users, participating in discussions, and writing reviews for books.

GOODREADS GIVEAWAYS

Goodreads is a great place to meet readers and fellow authors. It's a great place to promote your books and share your thoughts on other books. After all, the best writers are avid readers. Connect with other readers, and you've got something.

---

2 Just as this book was about to go to print, Amazon bought Goodreads and will soon be merging the two extensive databases together.

One of the many wonderful things about Goodreads is their giveaways. It can be a great way to find new readers. I've hosted giveaways for all my titles, at one time or another, and you'll have hundreds of entries in a matter of hours. This is a great central location for a book giveaway.

These giveaways are for physical paperback or hardback copies of the books, however, not for eBooks.

Well worth the little time it takes to create one.

Here's how:

1. Under *Explore* in the top menu, choose *Giveaways*
2. Near the top right, click on *List a Giveaway*
3. Choose the dates of the giveaway and put in the rest of the requested information, including a blurb about the book (copy/paste from what you have already written and saved to your desktop).
4. Click Save! That's easy!

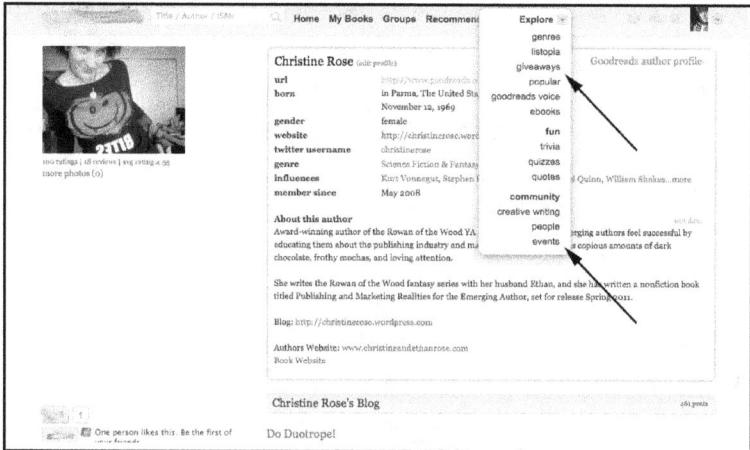

GOODREADS EVENTS

Similar to Facebook Events, Goodreads Events invites your Goodreads friends, although there is no special javascript code to do all at once. You can, however, select up to 60 at a time, but you can only invite 100 a day. You will have to come back day after day to invite the rest, so be sure to plan your event well in the future so you can get everyone invited.

Again, under *Explore* choose *Events* at the very bottom of that drop-down menu, then click on ***Add an event***. Fill in the requested information and click save.

There are so many Goodreads Events, just like there are so many Facebook Events, that you could get lost in the shuffle. But that's the way it is with all this marketing. Everyone is doing it for everything. That's why you have to be YOU --- find your niche and work it.

Work it, baby! Work it!

A QUICK NOTE ON TUMBLR

I've only recently joined Tumblr, as there are just so many hours in a day! I know people who swear by it, and it seems to be a good place to share and comment on a micro-blogging-type platform. If you can really work the network and get lots of followers and interact with everyone, as in any social network, Tumblr can really work for you. So can Pinterest or LinkedIn or GooglePlus or YouNameTheNextOne.

They all come down to this:
- Make personal connections
- Interact with the community
- Contribute to the discussions
- Be consistent and reliable
- Sprinkle sparingly with marketing info about your books
- Link back to your blog. It's your hub.

IMPORTANCE OF AUTOMATION

The more things you can automate, the better. This is the only way you'll have any time to actually write. As you're setting up your social networks, ensure that they are cross populating. That is, make sure every blog post is set to go to your Twitter feed, your Facebook profile, your Goodreads page (and others), and your Amazon Author Page.

When you place an update on your Facebook Fan Page, it should go directly to Twitter.

Use the tips through the above section on how to automate Tweets, and utilize Google Alerts to find content for you. Remember, this isn't all you need to do on Twitter, but it will give relevant content to your followers while you're busy writing your next masterpiece.

If you use TweetDeck, you can take 15 minutes out of your morning while you drink your coffee to schedule tweets throughout the day. This is especially helpful if it's a day you have a new blog post. But even if it's not, schedule several posts throughout the day that links to your blog. Find a different way to intrigue your Twitter followers enough that they click that link. While you're there, tell your followers just how good that coffee is...and maybe that you could use some chocolate. Strangely, many Twitter followers respond to food-themed tweets. They can relate. That's the key: finding something to which *your* readers can relate. That's how you build a following. Connect. If you can do this in a humorous or witty way, your following will grow even faster.

REALITY CHECK

According to a George Washington University[1] study, 89% of journalists turn to blogs for content, 65% turn to social networking, 52% turn to Twitter. Times have changed. Blogging and Social Media is the single best way to be seen and to build your own personal brand as an author.

---

1 "National Survey Finds Majority of Journalists Now Depend on Social Media for Story Research" George Washington University. 21 Jan 2010. Web. 07 Apr. 2011.

3. ONLINE PRESENCE

BLOGGING

Whether or not you choose to build your website around a blog or to have a traditional website, you really need a blog. This is one of the reasons it's best just to build your website around your blog, at least initially. You must update your blog at least once a week. Three times a week is better. Every day is even better, but that becomes quite time consuming when you also need to write.

Your blog is your hub. All social networking roads lead here.

Here your readers will learn about you, get samples of your writing, experience your voice, and find links to buy your books!

Ensure your author name is at the top of your blog. If at all possible, it should be part of the URL; e.g., yourname.wordpress.com. The name of your blog, or at the very least the subtitle, needs to have your author name in it. When people come to your blog, you want them to know who you are. You are creating a brand with your blog and all your online activity. BRAND YOUR NAME, not @sexywriter69. As social networking expert Kristen Lamb says, I can't go to Amazon or the bookstore and buy Sexy Writer69's book.

BRAND. YOUR. NAME.

Everything you do online should be directing potential readers back to your blog. This is your marketing hub. Twitter, Facebook, Goodreads, and your marketing materials should all point back to your blog.

Have I mentioned? This is your HUB.

WHY BLOG?

- It will get you in the habit of writing content frequently, on a deadline, and then moving on. This hones skills essential for the working author.
- It will help you find your voice.
- It will help with your SEO stats (Search Engine Optimization), just another way for people to find you.
- Blogging will improve your chances for success because it will increase your visibility and your potential readership.
- It makes you look like a professional, as long as you keep it professional. This means to leave out personal details and drama. Although, as a romance writer under O. M. Grey, I started writing about relationships struggles and challenges, objectively at first, then gradually more personal, and it significantly increased my readership. I mean, significantly. I went from under 100 views a day to averaging between 350 and 500 views a day. There is a fine line between writing your passions and staying professional.

- Blogging puts the author in control of product and platform. Build your platform through your blog.
- Don't blog about writing or marketing or networking unless you're trying to sell a book on writing or marketing or networking.
- Write content that is interesting to you and will be interesting and/or helpful to your reader. This blog is meant to CONNECT you with your reader. Everything you do online via social networks or your blog is to connect you with your readers.

REALITY CHECK

It would be best not to use your blog as a journal about your life. As of now, you are an unknown author and no one cares who you are or what you're doing with your days. In other words, your life doesn't matter to cyberspace. Not yet. What you have to say, especially if you say it in an entertaining or informative way, is of interest. Write to your strengths. If you're not funny, don't try to be.
Or, learn to be.

Start blogging NOW, not after your book comes out. This goes for all the social and online networking. Build those relationships before you have something to sell them. Let them all get to know you, then they won't mind when you tell them you have a new book out. They will be excited along with you.

WHAT TO BLOG ABOUT?

Whatever catches your fancy. Blog about technology or crocheting or dogs or frisbee golf. Sprinkle with minimal stuff about your life and writing. Publish short fiction on your blog. Podcast. Vlog. Write what's in your heart or your mind. Write about a current event. Opinions. Just blog, and blog often. Make the writing interesting. As a writer, your blog might be the first thing your reader sees.

Above all, keep the negativity to a minimum. People don't need another downer in their lives, although through my rough times I've posted some pretty dark stuff, and I've increased my readership. There are a lot of people in pain. Still, this worked because people knew me before the trauma, so they were with me through it. Besides, I don't see those things as "negative." When I say "negative" I mean bad mouthing people, complaining, being catty or petty. Intolerant or spewing hatred. If you're discussing dark topics like rape, domestic violence, or mental illness, those are very important conversations to have, even though they might not be "positive" or happy ones. They are necessary, and we as a society have been silent about it for too long. If it fits with your fiction and your demographic, write about it.

Be yourself, but be positive. Just when you think no one is paying attention to what you do (and believe me, you will think that), you'll put up something negative or catty or petty and you'll suddenly see how many people are watching. I've seen it ruin careers before they even got started. Most people on the internet lurk, but they'll come out in force to help you embarrass yourself. Dirty laundry doesn't belong on the web. It will always come back to haunt you.

People are going to buy your book because they know and like YOU. Remember: 950 books a day. What makes yours unique? YOU. Now show the world who you are. Just like when writing fiction, don't *TELL* them (by journaling about your life), **SHOW** them by writing engaging articles about cats or cooking or relationships or whatever catches your fancy. Something that can be tied into your book is the best, but it isn't necessary.

- DO NOT blog from your character's point of view. I've done this. Again, no one cares. No one knows your characters yet, so **no one cares**...yet.
- DO NOT blog sections from your novel. See above.
- DO write blogs on topics you're passionate about, but make it on topic.

Think of your targeted audience. For romance authors, this might be women between the ages of 18 and 65. What is that demographic interested in? Here are some ideas: love, dating, families, children, gardening, cooking, knitting, sewing, sex, relationships, communicating with your spouse, etc.

What if you are a mystery author? Chances are your target audience likes to watch shows like *Castle* and *Bones* and *CSI*. Write about true crime. Write about forensic science. Write about blood splatter. Review other books.

YA? Remember that teens aren't likely the ones reading your blog. And if you write MG (Middle Grade), they most certainly are not reading your blog. Write to the BUYER; i.e., the parents and the teachers.

Paranormal Romance? Write about ghosts and vampires and aliens. Psychics, Ouija boards, demons, witches, anything supernatural. Likely, your readers will love those things as well.

EXERCISE:

Get out a piece of paper right now and brainstorm for fifteen minutes on blog topics. Better yet, don't stop until you have 100, then pick the top 15.

WHEN? WHEN AM I GOING TO DO ALL THIS?

One of the coolest things about blogging is that you can do it in advance. Take Sunday morning, for example, and write three blogs. They don't have to be long, just between 300 and 1000 words or so. You should be able to write three blogs in three hours, especially if you have that nice long brainstorming list of blog topics done in the previous exercise. Now schedule each blog to publish later that week. Monday, Wednesday, and Friday, for example. You can even have different themed days.

On http://christinerose.wordpress.com, I started the blog by publishing industry-related posts on Monday; focused on emerging indie authors, their books, or the craft of writing on Wednesdays for #WW; and Fridays were reserved for Social Networking and Marketing posts. That's changed over time, and that's okay. Now I post fiction podcasts and book reviews, and instead of those three initial topics on three separate days, they all get one day a week. For example, one week might be on the publishing industry, the next on marketing or the writing craft. I have one business day a week, one fun day with the podcasts, and one book review day. This inspires me to keep up with my reading, as it's essential for a writer to read, and incorporate that into my blogging. It also works for Amazon reviews and Goodreads reviews. Each review you post on a book leads someone back to your blog.

Your blog is your marketing hub.

On O. M. Grey's blog (http://omgrey.wordpress.com), I started by focosing on a Steampunk-themed artist, band, author, or event for #SteamTuesday, called "Steampunk Spotlight "on Tuesdays, but now that I'm moving away from Steampunk-specific fiction, I'm posting book reviews on some Tuesdays, Steampunk Spotlights on others, and updates about my career sprinkled throughout. Wednesday is time for Hump Day, discussing relationships, love, and sex; and Freaky Fridays are for all things paranormal, poetry, short stories, or fiction podcasts.

When you schedule your blog to publish on a given day, you will have also ensured that the new post will be announced on Facebook, Twitter, Goodreads, etc., as you set all this up earlier through WordPress. So while you're writing your novel Monday morning, you have fresh content automatically posting on your blog and all your social networks. Then, when you take a mid-morning chocolate break, because, let's face it, chocolate is essential for the working author, check each network, your email, and your blog. Don't spend longer than 15 minutes doing this before going back to writing your book.

BLOG COMMENTS

You must respond to every comment you get. In fact, that's the purpose of blogs: to inspire people and create community discussions. Write your blogs in an open forum. Perhaps ask questions for your reader to answer. Ask them for help on a topic or opinion. Invite them to participate in a discussion, and when they do comment, you absolutely must answer that comment in a timely manner. This way you keep the discussion going. I utilize the WordPress app on my iPhone, so when someone comments, it pops up in a push notification. It's never long before I respond to a blog comment.

As in everything, it will take time for you to build a readership and a community, but you will likely see an increase in site views and comments within the first month. If you're getting the blog hits but not the comments, then look at your posts. See what you can do to inspire more interaction. You must give readers a reason to come to your blog, and more importantly, a reason to come back. Quizzes. Questions. Opinions. In your blogging, you must serve the reader first[1].

TAGS & CATEGORIES

Tagging your blog, as well as organizing them into categories, is very important. Categories help readers find previous posts under a certain topic, but the Tags are what help readers find your blog via search engines.

Keep categories at a minimum, perhaps four or five at the most. Category examples are much more general, like "Fiction Podcasts," "Romance & Relationships," "Writing," "Life with Dogs," or whatever you're going to be writing about.

Tags are micro-specific. If my fiction podcast is a short story about a woman who falls in love with a book, these might be my tags:

olivia grey, o. m. grey, omgrey, writer, author, blogger, blog, podcast, fiction, fiction podcast, audio fiction, love, romance, relationship, fantasy, book, short story, short fiction, for the love of a book, sex, new york, rain, taxi cab...

Go on a tagging frenzy! The more tags the better.

Every single post should have your name in the tags as well as the word "author" and "writer" and whatever topic you most often write about.

Every. Single. Post.

Then think of as many tags as you can and tag away. What's hot in the news? Can you somehow fit that into a post, then into the tags? Or

---

1 For a list of writers who blog regularly, see the Appendix

something from pop culture? One of my most-viewed posts is on Mal and Inara from *Firefly*. My all-time top viewed posts are "Pathology of a Commitmentphobe" and "PTSD from Emotional Abuse." Truly amazing how many views those two posts have had and continue to have.

Don't scrimp on the tags. This is how search engines find you. Once I learned this little tidbit, my daily views doubled. Overnight.

EXERCISE:

Brainstorm for 15 minutes. Write down as many words you can think of that describe your book(s), you, your (planned) blog content. These are the tags you'll use in every post. Then also insert tags specific to each post on top of that. Visit omgrey.wordpress.com for a tagging example.

> ### TIP
> In your widgets, add a "tag cloud" to your sidebar. This will enable readers to find posts based on your tags.

Finding things to write about, fresh content, is often the most difficult part of keeping a blog. Once I have an idea, the words flow, but for me, coming up with that idea is the hardest part. That's where that brainstorming exercise comes in handy. Best bet: write out fifteen to twenty posts and schedule them over a three-month period before ever making your blog live, then you'll have some wiggle room.

Here is an example blog post about writing from the heart:

"Stay True to Your Reader, or Sell Out?"
In the writing business, we often get conflicting advice from our readers, other writers, and industry professionals like agents and editors. Agents advise us to write what's in our hearts, but they can only sell what the editors want. The editors want more of what is already selling, limiting their risk in this fast-changing business. I've overheard readers in bookstores scoff at yet another new vampire novel. Other writers have told me that

vampires are overdone; prophecies, tired. Yet this is exactly the opposite of the advice from New York. Vampires sell, so they want more vampires. Steampunk is popular, so they want more Steampunk.

They are the ones writing the checks.

This is the paradox. For what is in our hearts is not always what New York wants to buy. It's not always what readers want to read.

And the bills keep coming.

Do we stay true to our readers? True to ourselves? Or do we sell out, as it were, to what the industry wants in some desperate and usually futile attempt to make a living?

First of all, being true to our readers isn't part of this choice. Readers either relate to our written word or they don't. The only choice for writers is either to write what's in one's heart, New York be damned, or to sell out and try to write something that New York might want to buy.

For those of us who are full time writers, as the bills pile up and the money remains scarce, we sometimes lose our way and try to force something, somehow merge the two. We scramble for a way to write what's in our hearts, what our soul demands to be released, in a fashion that will also be attractive to editors, journals, magazines—anyone who can help us make ends meet.

But in the words of Kurt Vonnegut, "Write to please just one person. If you open a window and make love to the world, so to speak, your story will get pneumonia."

And so on.

(Originally posted on C&E blog[1], January 25, 2011.)

---

1 http://www.christineandethanrose.com/blog

I wrote a similar, more emotional post on my alter-ego O. M. Grey's blog[2]. This was originally posted after a series I did on relationships and loss:

"Writing for Survival"

The past three months of my life have been primarily spent on this one task: survival. It's probably safe to say that anyone reading this has experienced the pain that comes with the loss of a love, either by breakup, divorce, or death–abandonment in its many forms. Loss is a task that is shared and forcibly undertaken by nearly every human being at one time or another, often multiple times, throughout their lives.

Healing, becoming me again, became my full-time job where my entire focus was devoted to not just making it through the day, but through the next five minutes. Although the loss of a love and a cherished friendship (one which despite my best efforts, I have not given up hope at renewing, fixing somehow) can be crippling, life continues.

Writers write for many reasons–to give voice to an opinion, to inform, to entertain–but ultimately we write as a means of survival. Emotional survival. Spiritual survival. And even financial survival, because beneath it all–the pain, the doubt, the regret, the fear–mortgages, bills, and responsibilities remain.

Life continues.

The sun rises. The bills come. The blank page screams for content. The deafening chatter of endless Tweets speaks to everyone but you. None of this stops.

Everything I wrote during this time, from the poetry to the short stories to the relationship articles, was inspired by the struggle of a failing relationship and, ultimately, the loss of it. But that's

2 http://omgrey.wordpress.com

not quite accurate. It was more than inspired by the events, it became a way to work through the grief, the confusion, and the unending analysis of where it went so wrong.

Writing became my catharsis, a way to cope with the heartbreak and the suffocating emptiness that followed.

Interestingly, the poems and the posts on relationships got more attention, comments, and retweets than anything I had ever posted before. I wrote from the heart and readers responded.

Writers must write what's in our hearts. We have no choice. I wrote what was in my heart even when my heart felt shattered, and readers responded. When readers can identify with the words on the page, when one can bare their soul and have others empathize, that is the very definition of success.

(Originally posted on Caught in the Cogs[1] on January 25, 2011)

The most interesting thing about the ongoing O. M. Grey experiment is that she enables me to talk about things Christine Rose wouldn't normally talk about. One of those things, as previously mentioned, is the articles on relationships and alternative lifestyles. I noticed a significant increase in my daily stats when I'd talk about relationships, break-up, heartbreak, and polyamory. So significant in fact, I now dedicate a day every week to continuing this trend. I've gained hundreds of new readers because of this, and I've sold more than a few books because of it, too.

Find what works for you. This is where analytics and tracking your marketing efforts will help. It shows when you are connecting with your readers and when you are not.

If you find one blog is getting more views than others, consider writing more on that topic.

---

1 http://omgrey.wordpress.com

OTHER IDEAS & TIPS FOR YOUR BLOG

- **Guest posts.** Get other authors/industry professionals to write a guest blog for you. Write a guest blog for them.
- **Reviews**. Meet some authors online via Twitter or wherever, and tell them you would like to review their book. Most authors will send you a free book or at least a free eBook. Write a review and post it on your blog (as well as on Amazon, Goodreads, LibraryThing, etc.). Then promote it via Twitter and Facebook and the rest of your networks. The author will promote it, too, driving traffic to your blog. I met some great authors who became dear friends by doing this. Then hopefully, they will help promote you.

Cross-promotion is GOLD.

- If you write romance, try posting a sexy picture of the day. Write about constructing sex scenes. What to do and what not to do. Write about sprucing up your sex life. Write about connecting with your spouse, rekindling the romance, romantic tips and ideas, etc.
- **Connect with readers** by using inclusive pronouns like we, our, etc. Strive to connect with readers over impressing them. Every bit of marketing is meant to connect with your audience.
- **VERY IMPORTANT: Be Consistent.**
- Sign up for WordPress's Blog a Day or Blog a Week challenge[2]. They post daily topics to get your creative juices flowing. This will help you come up with content until you've got your blogging chops working and writing daily.
- **Spend time on other author's blogs**, and you'll see what they write about. Comment on those blogs, putting your URL in the comment-author form. As in all of Social Networking, the best way to get people to read and comment on your blog is to read and comment on theirs.

Quid pro quo, Clarise.

---

2 http://dailypost.wordpress.com/

BLOG TOURS

A blog tour is when an author visits a different blog every day for a specific length of time. This can be a few days or a few weeks, all depending on how much time and work (and how much exposure) you want to put into it.

Start by finding at least a dozen blogs that fit with your topic. If you write YA or fantasy, please visit our blog tour archives[1] to get links to some blogs. If you write fantasy or paranormal romance, definitely try to get on BittenByBooks[2] for your online release party. They are amazing and have a huge following. Each of those blogs (or those from your own list) have blogrolls, a list of links they like or frequent. Often these links are of similar blogs. Just take a day or two and explore, making a list of the top fifty or sixty blogs that fit your book. Start querying the top ones; i.e., the ones with the most activity (comments and discussion).

Decide when and how long your blog tour will be. When you query, tell them who you are along with a short blurb about your book. Remember those things I had you write at the beginning of the marketing section? Here is one place you use them. Be sure to suggest a date in your query. For example, "Would you have Friday, April 22nd available?" Or, alternatively, give them two or three choices: "I have Friday 4/22, Wednesday 4/27, or Thursday 4/28 open. Which would work best for you?"

As you go, keep a blog post in the draft stage on your own blog planning your blog tour with links. This way you can see where there are holes and which days are already filled. Do this as you go, and it's less work than trying to put it all together at the end.

There are several things you can do on a blog tour.

- Write a guest post.
- Do an interview.
- Have them write a book review.

---

1 Links to archives on the "Resources" page at http://christinerose.wordpress.com
2 http://bittenbybooks.com -- Site dedicated to author interviews, book reviews, contests, and online release parties, which is a date set where you hold a virtual party. Invite everyone using social networks, then show up and interact with fans. Coordinate this with reviews, a blog tour, and other events to get the most out of it.

- Post a vlog. Post a podcast.
- Hold a contest.
- Giveaway eBook and/or paperback copies of your book.
- Offer a free short story, or, better yet, half a free short story with the other half on your own blog, diving traffic there
- Excerpt from your book
- Make a blog tour banner, like the one below, to put on your blog and on each stop during the tour. Have this banner link back to your blog tour schedule.

Use your imagination, and most importantly, have fun!

When it's time for your blog tour, market like crazy. The day before your tour starts, post your blog tour schedule on your blog and invite readers to follow you over the next two weeks, or however long your tour lasts. Post where you'll be on your blog each day and what you'll be discussing (or what's happening like a review, vlog, etc.). Ensure each daily blog post links back to your overall blog tour schedule. Tweet it. Post it on Facebook. Create a Facebook Event. Create a Goodreads Event. Utilize all the networks you've spent so much time creating NOW. You'll be so glad all that automation is in place, as it will reduce the places to post.

Work those networks. Ask top fans for specific action, like to comment on a specific blog or share with their networks.

Be available several times during the day to respond to comments. Readers want to interact with the author, so be available to do so. When you're on a blog tour, you should be doing little else but marketing, responding to readers, and then marketing some more.

> ## IMPORTANT
> Don't hold a blog tour until your book is released and available to purchase from Amazon, at least. People often make impulse purchases, and you don't want to miss out on this.
> They won't remember next week.

CONTESTS

Don't waste your time. Really. Especially if you're holding a random contest. Contests work best in the context of something larger, like a blog tour.

Actually, I've spoken with authors who have had a moderate success with contests, so it might be beneficial to you, even though they've never been worth the money spent for me.

Regardless, you must remember the four maxims of marketing:

1. People are Broke
2. People are Lazy
3. People are Busy
4. Above all...it's a Numbers Game

Once you have 10,000+ followers on Twitter and are getting over 10,000 hits on your blog every week, then you might have a successful contest. The more readers you have, the more will enter your contest. The more places you advertise your contest, the more will enter your contest.

Contests used to be a great way of reaching potential readers and raising awareness around your book; however, in case I haven't mentioned it, times are changing. Now there are so many giveaways, consumers know that it's just another way to sell them something. They know. They're tired of it. They don't have time for it.

So unless you have a built in following or are offering a *really* great prize (like a $500+ iPad), you won't get many entries. Even with a high-ticket item like an iPad, you still won't get too many. Just mention the word iPad on Twitter, and you'll be bombarded with several SPAMMING tweets on how you can win an iPad. Giving away an iPad might sound like a great prize, but you'll be very lucky to get enough book sales to cover the cost. You'll be very, very lucky.

I tried this a few years ago by giving away a Kindle 2, back when they were still $360. This was before I learned what I now know about community and marketing. I made it too complicated to enter, so I got about five entries. So many people in 2009 didn't even know what a Kindle was. Fortunately, BittenByBooks[1] picked up the contest and co-hosted it. They simplified it some and they have a HUGE following. I even made a silly video called "Don't You Want A Kindle?" to the tune of The Human League's "Don't You Want Me, Baby?" You can still see it over on TheTuberRose[2] on YouTube. Overall, I think I got about 250 entries. Book sales barely covered the cost of the Kindle, which means we sold about 25 copies. The winner, chosen by Random.org to make it fair, got her brand new Kindle 2. I asked her about a month later how she was enjoying it, and she replied that it was "in a box around here somewhere." I was heartbroken.

Since, even with all I've learned, I still made the same mistake last year. Due to the break in marketing because of the personal issues I've eluded to, I recently held a blog tour with those dreaded contests. I spent $150 in prizes, like a Kindle and Amazon Gift Cards, not to mention shipping and the cost of the books given away. From that blog tour, readers purchased four (yes, 4) Kindle books at $2.99 and three (3)

1 http://bittenbybooks.com
2 http://www.youtube.com/watch?v=5uBHUkwrFXw

paperbacks at $12.95. So, for $150 out of pocket and countless hours of my time, I made under $50 in sales, and that's not net minus the price of printing the book, that's gross.

That's reality.

Still, if you have the following and you've effectively built your community, this can work for you and your book. Or, if you do this during a blog tour and you have managed to get on several high profile blogs, a contest could work. It really does raise your visibility and finds you new readers, so if you look at the expense as just part of your marketing budget, this could be a good long-term investment. Just don't expect contests to pay for themselves. They rarely do.

Try building up to the level of a Kindle or iPad. You might consider mini contests like a $5 Amazon gift card when you reach x# of followers on Twitter or on your FB Fan Page.

KISS.

Amazon gift cards work best, even just $5 or $25. Copies of your book rarely work well because people generally have more things to read than they have time to read them. And, remember, they just don't care yet (unless it's on Goodreads, then you'll have hundreds of entries). They don't know you yet. However, on a blog tour, giving away a copy of your book could increase your readership, especially if you post a teaser chapter or excerpt on one of your guest posts to get them interested.

PODCASTING

Similar to vlogging, some authors podcast their books, short stories, or other relevant information to gather followers and potential readers. One Blue Moose Press author, Paul E. Cooley, has gained a huge following through his podcasting efforts. I have, too.

I shied away from podcasting for years because I was concerned about the amount of time I'd spend in editing. Coming off video editing, which is grossly time-consuming, there was already too much time spent on marketing for me to spent four hours editing a 30-minute segment.

Turns out, it didn't take that much editing. I was thinking about sound effects and soundtracks and high production value, but when I started podcasting I realized that it can be very, very bare-bones. An intro, an outro[1], my voice and that's it. I edit as I record, stopping when I make a mistake, going back to the point of the mistake, and starting again. I can record a 30-minute podcast in 45 minutes to an hour, and podcasting has brought me a whole new readership! I started podcasting blog posts on Publishing & Marketing, after the release of the first edition of this book on http://christinerose.wordpress.com, as well as blog posts on relationships and polyamory on http://omgrey.wordpress.com. When things got so difficult to focus, I added fiction podcasts on both blogs, podcasting a serialized novel on each. *Rowan of the Wood* and *Witch on the Water* on Christine's and *Avalon Revisited*[2] and *The Zombies of Mesmer,* as well as short fiction and poetry, on Olivia's. It's like a free audio book, serialized.

People love podcasts, either nonfiction or fiction, because it's something they can listen to on their commute to work or while they're doing something else.

If you plan to podcast, get a decent microphone and record quality sound. People will absolutely not listen to bad sound. I record on a Zoom H2. It cost me about $100.

If you have a Mac, you can podcast directly in GarageBand. There are even online videos to teach you how to do so. On PCs, there are several free or low cost audio editing suites. Just Google it. Also, there are plenty of sites around the internet that will help you get started in podcasting. Award-winning podcaster Tee Morris wrote the book *Podcasting for Dummies*. I had the wonderful opportunity to work with Tee on a podcast anthology for his Steampunk novel. Olivia wrote and recorded "Dust on the Davenport," a short story set in Tee's world. After it was podcasted, Olivia gained several new readers just because of that short story podcast. It gave both me and her the podcasting bug.

---

1 Intro & Outro = music leading into and out of your podcast. Like a theme song.

2 *Avalon Revisited* has since been picked up by an audio-book publisher, so the podcast is no longer on iTunes or Olivia's blog. See what can happen!

There are great tutorials online on how to utilize your blog with Feedburner to get your podcast in the pockets of thousands via iTunes. Google it.

REVIEWS

Reviews are a wonderful way to raise visibility of your book. There are countless number of review blogs on the web, and you should make a list of the top blogs that discuss and review books like yours. Query the top ten first. Ideally, you want a blog that contains a lot of regular activity. Look at the comments. If they consistently have discussions beneath their posts, they likely have a nice following. But even those blogs that don't have much discussion can certainly raise your book's visibility on the web.

Most blogs will have an "about" page or "contact" page. When possible, address the contact by name when emailing your query. For organizational purposes, put your book title and the name of the blog in the subject line. This will help you and the recipient find the conversation in their inbox. Additionally, send a query to the Midwest Book Review. They are one of the premiere review sites for independent books.

Be sure to send out ARC (advance review copies) at least a month or two in advance if you're planning a big release splash and blog tour. Then reviewers will have a chance to read and review your book in time for your release. If you are published through a NYBB, they should take care of most of this, but don't hesitate to do some legwork of your own. Remember, it's up to you to promote your book. When you have a blog tour planned with review requests, get your publisher to send out the ARCs. They should be more than happy to do so, and review copies with a NYBB should be limitless. Some independent publishers will put a cap on review copies, which is one of the many reasons not to go with an indie press. Ask all these questions up front.

Never pay for a review. This goes back to never paying someone to publish your book (unless you consciously choose to go the vanity publishing route after weighing all your options) and never paying an agent a reading fee. Unfortunately, two of the most prestigious review journals are now preying on indie authors. *Kirkus* and *Publishers Weekly* each have a program that, for a fee, will review your book for their publication. Don't do it.

Another *huge* DON'T: don't respond to negative reviews. Ever. Just let them go. They will be forgotten by next week unless you keep them alive. I've seen authors mocked online (extensively) because of their responses to a bad review. Let it go.

Keep breathing life into the good reviews.

It's also quite beneficial to get reviews on Amazon.com, and it's okay to ask specifically for these reviews. A lot of readers just don't think

---

PLEASE NOTE:

If you want to try and get your book reviewed by major reviewers (Publishers Weekly, Kirkus, etc.), they will want a book at least four months before publication, so plan ahead.

---

about writing a review. It really never crosses their minds. This is when it's okay to ask them for a review.

When you sell a book at an event, right after you sign it to them, say, "If you like it, please consider leaving a review on Amazon.com and Goodreads. It would be so helpful and appreciated." Or something to that effect. Similarly, when you give away free copies online, like through a blog tour, get something out of those free copies! When you email them the PDF or Amazon gift card or whatever, ask them for a review.

I've gotten into the habit of asking for reviews from my Top Fans and even on Facebook from time to time. Targeted marketing with specific requests work so very well.

As in all marketing, you can't do this every week or you'll become annoying. These things can only be asked of cultivated relationships or when there is a perceived debt to you, like you just gave them something for free or signed their book. There isn't really a debt, but they feel lucky and special in that moment, so ask them for this little thing in return.

Many people are nervous about leaving reviews becuase they don't spell well or they think they can't write. I always add: "Just a sentence or two would be so helpful. It doesn't have to be long."

Once your book gets 50 reviews on Amazon.com, it goes into a higher-level search algorithm. Work it!

PAID ADVERTISEMENTS

As far as I'm concerned, they are never worth the money. For paid ads to work, they have to be everywhere the consumer looks for weeks or months, sometimes over a year. And even then the ROI[1] is very low. Don't waste your money, not even on the Facebook ads or the Google AdWords, both set us as pay-per-click. Still not worth it, not until you're already a recognized name.

Remember, you are an emerging author. No one knows who you are yet. Sure, Stephen King could have an ad that he has a new book, and it would work great, but all consumers will see with your ad is "Joe Shmoe has written another book. Joy."

That's if they even see that much.

Most ads go completely unseen. People block out advertisements as easily as they scan through commercials on their DVR.

Marketing, much like the publishing industry, is changing. The old models no longer work effectively. Now it's about WOM (Word of Mouth). That has the highest ROI, and that is how your networks will find your book, especially if your book is not on the front kiosk in every Barnes & Noble across the country. Which, let's face it, even if you are published with a NYBB, is quite unlikely. Those kiosks are reserved for the recognizable author names, not an emerging author. Because, remember, those kiosks cost the publisher a lot of money, and they're not going to put anything there that is not a sure sale.

---

1 ROI = return on investment

4. GENRE CONVENTIONS & OTHER VENUES

"Expect Superman: Working the SFF Con"

You've just gotten your first speculative fiction work published, and now you need to get it out there to potential readers. Whether you are self-published, published by an independent press, or published in New York, marketing your book is up to you. Since you are a writer of speculative fiction (SciFi/Fantasy, or SFF), you have an excellent option to get your book directly into the hands of your niche market: SFF Conventions.

Fantasy conventions occur nearly every weekend somewhere in the USA, so it all depends how far you want to travel and how much you want to spend marketing your book. Over the past two and a half years, I've participated in many SFF Conventions (Cons), art shows, Celtic Festivals, and Renaissance Faires to promote my fantasy novels and my Steampunk romance novel.

SFF cons can be a lot of fun for a working author if one sets their expectations at the right level.

Superman. Expect Superman: at least one middle-aged Superman in sky blue spandex and a very tight red speedo.

No kidding.

In fact, you will see many amazing costumes at SFF cons. These people take their fantasy seriously, and that's exactly the kind of person you want to be passionate about your book(s). It would behoove you to dress up in a costume as well, especially if you write Steampunk. It's still new enough that you will get countless people stopping at your table just to take your picture or ask you about how you are dressed. Perfect opportunity to pitch your book and hand them a bookmark full of your information and social networks. I've sold more than a few books just because of my corset and bustle.

Expect long hours. Most SFF cons run 10-12 hours a day, and that's not including the parties in the evenings, where much of the networking takes place.

Expect little time to eat. Bring snacks to nibble on because invariably as soon as you take a bite a customer will magically appear.

Expect to barely break even on expenses, if you're lucky. Fantasy conventions can be expensive to do, but a working author must look at them as a marketing expense. You will have to cover travel (air or gas), hotel, and the table fee. Table fees in the Artist Alley (for artists and authors) generally run anywhere from $25 to $200. If you break even, you're doing very well. If you make a profit, assume it is an anomaly and don't expect it to happen again.

TIPS

Signage & Table Display

- Make sure your table is attractive and professional.

- Bring a table covering, as many cons do not provide one. This can be as simple as a few yards of black velveteen.

- Having some sort of poster, vinyl banner, or a window shade-type display is essential, and they are well worth the investment for all your marketing events. A window shade display can be pricey and a poster can be bulky. Vinyl banners are great because they pack well. If you can make some sort of collapsible stand (I have one made from copper pipe & connectors), a vinyl banner can work well as a backdrop.

Check out etsy.com for handmade displays and support other independent artists.

- Create a vertical display on the table itself with a book stand or easels, as it's much more eye catching.

- Have a lot of books. I mean it. You want stacks and stacks of books. You do not want to sell out. Selling out looks really great on a press release, but selling out means you could've sold more books had you been better prepared.

- If you can, have something other than books for people to look at. It's very easy for people to see a table of books (especially if it's all just one book) and say to themselves "I'm not looking for a new book." If there are other things to look at, especially if they relate to your book in some way, it slows them down enough to look. Then you can pitch. Also, if they all relate to your book, then you have a great segue. Create some art or buttons or something. If you aren't artistic in that way, then team up with an artist friend.

Engage Potential Fans

- Make eye contact.

- Have something ready to stop them if they look over at you for more than one second. Many people need to be engaged to stop. They don't know you, so you have to introduce yourself and tell them who you are.

- Start with something, perhaps a question. I've heard authors ask "Are you a reader?" or "Are you familiar with Steampunk?" If they are in costume, start by complimenting their outfit. They likely put a lot of work into it. Even ask if you can have your picture taken with them. Then you can hand them a card and tell them you will post the picture on your blog.

- Then pitch your book. Have your pitch down. You will say it a dozen times an hour, if you're lucky. Short, to the point. You want them to pick up your book and look further.

- Tell them that you will happily sign it for them. Most celebrities at cons charge a fee for their autographs, so many con-goers are thrilled to get an author-signed book for no extra charge. People LOVE author-signed books. Several times I've had a new reader tell me that it was their first author-signed book. They will never forget that.

- Hand out business cards, or preferably, bookmarks. Bookmarks are less likely to wind up in the recycling or on a pile of other cards on someone's desk. Bookmarks will at least end up in a book, which ensures that the reader will see your information more than just once. One side of the bookmark should have the cover art of your book(s), the other should have your social networks (including Twitter, Facebook, Goodreads, etc,), your website/blog, your email address and a short synopsis. Even if they don't buy a book, make sure everyone walks away with one of your cards. Again, I use NextDayFlyers. Their prices cannot be beat. I find their 1/8 page "club flyer" and "bookmarks" work quite well for this.

("Expect Superman" was originally posted on the Best Damn Creative Writing Blog, January 10, 2011.)

In addition to a dealer or artist alley table, try to get on some of the convention's programming: panels, readings, autograph sessions, etc. The purpose of cons is to be visible, not to make money. Fantasy Conventions are far from money-makers for emerging authors, in fact, count yourself very lucky if you break even. Cons are a place to connect with fans. ***True fans;*** i.e., fanatics. The people who go to cons are very, very serious about their fiction, gaming, and pop culture.

Very. Very. Serious.

You will likely have a con-goer or two trap you at your table, telling you the ins and outs of *Doctor Who* and how Tennant truly got the deep-seated pathos of love and loss after 900 years of life, or they'll tell you in great detail the difference between Trekkies and Trekkers.

In Klingon.

Others will describe the book series they're developing or show you their teddy bear collection which they take everywhere and refer to as their "family."

I'm really not kidding.

Smile, nod, and be polite. These are, after all, your potential fans. But do not ask questions; it will just prolong the encounter. Don't hesitate to say, "Excuse me for a moment," even if you interrupt them, to take care of a potential customer. After all, you are there to make a living and get your book in front of as many people as possible.

Perhaps the best thing about genre conventions, aside from the fans, is the networking. You will meet with other authors and artists trying to do what you're doing. Bond with them and create a network of professionals. Promote their books and art on Twitter and your other social networks. Keep in touch over Facebook, share notes, and cross promote.

Cross-Promotion is GOLD.

As you make a name for yourself, graduate to being a guest of honor. Then the convention will pay for your hotel and/or travel, plus give you that vendor table space for free in exchange for using your name, your presence, and your participation in their programming.

In addition to SFF Cons, which are best for Speculative Fiction writers, there are other creative venues where you can promote your book. Here is just a short list of examples:
- Farmers' Markets
- Celtic Festivals (these are our best shows. Since our YA books are based in Celtic Mythology, it worked well. Primarily through

these Celtic Festivals is how we sold so many books that first year.)
- Renaissance Festivals (if you write fantasy)
- Art Festivals
- Book Festivals (the Texas Book Festival in Austin, TX was where we sold the 2nd most books in a weekend. Festivals, especially the big ones, are where readers go to find new books.)
- Street Fairs
- Metaphysical Shows (especially if you write paranormal content)
- You can also give talks to a various number of places. See Denniger Bolton's essay in the Author Essay section for how he successfully does this.
- Brainstorm to think of more venues for your particular book.

MARKETING TIPS & TRICKS
ACCEPT CREDIT CARDS

You will lose sales if you don't accept credit cards. Fortunately, there is a wonderful device called SQUARE, and you can find out more about it at http://squareup.com. PayPal now has a card reader like this, too. Here is a post I wrote about the Square Merchant Services for The Best Damn Creative Writing Blog:

TOTALLY SQUARE

A few weeks ago at a fantasy convention, a colleague turned me on to SQUARE. And it is the coolest. thing. ever.

Ethan and I have been on the road promoting and selling our books for over three years now. In doing so, we had to get a merchant account, because without one you're unable to take credit cards. If you can't take credit cards, you lose out on sales. We signed up for a merchant account through Total Merchant Services, and they've been rather good to us overall. But it is normally very expensive to have a merchant account. Prohibitively so unless you're using it close to full time. There is a monthly fee. There is a wireless fee, which is a necessity to be able to take credit cards at events and on-the-go. There is a minimum amount you must charge in percentages every month or they charge you anyway. There is a 3 (!) year contract, and if you don't cancel your contract within a specific amount of time before it expires, it automatically renews. To get out of a contract is several hundred dollars.

Not good. Especially since we're now doing fewer shows than when we started.

Enter Square…my life saver.

SQUARE is a merchant account with no monthly fees. No contracts. You don't have to buy the credit card machine, as they send it to you for FREE. (And it's so small you can carry it in your pocket.) You don't even have to buy the app. It's FREE, TOO!

The Square card reader currently works with iPhone, iPad, iPod Touch, and Android phones. I don't doubt that Blackberry will soon follow. When you set up your account online at squareup. com, you will connect your Square account with your bank account. They will make two small deposits (similar to what PayPal does) into your account and then ask you to verify those amounts. After that, you're done!

They're percentage for swiped transactions is 2.75%, which is comparable to other merchant accounts. With Square, we can now take American Express in addition to Visa, MC, and Discover, something we cannot do with TMS without significant fees.

And it's EASY (and so very cool). You swipe the card, enter the amount, and then the customer digitally signs your iPhone (or iPad, etc) with their finger! You can email or text them a receipt on the spot (Square even remembers the email associated with a specific CC if they've used Square in the past).

You will receive an email detailing the transaction along with your running Square balance. Approximately three business days later, the funds are in your verified bank account, also comparable to the time other merchant accounts take to get funds to you, only Square has no batching fees like other merchant accounts do.

Yep. Super. fricken. cool.

The only limitation I've seen is that they only allow $1000 worth of transactions per week. If you go over $1000 in a week, the excess will be deposited within 30 days. If you regularly go over $1000, Square will increase your weekly spending limit.

It will even track your cash receipts. Score.

Every working author should have one. Don't have a smart phone? Time to invest in one. It will be your portable book-marketing machine. Seriously. It's a necessity for a working author. More on that in a forthcoming post.

(This post first appeared on the Best Damn Creative Writing Blog, March 25, 2011[1])

Accepting credit cards is a must. With the Square or with PayPal's new card reader, it's easy. It's smart. It's essential. They work on your iPad or smart phone, so you can take credit cards anywhere, anytime.

No smart phone? Time to get one.

IMPORTANCE OF A SMART PHONE

If you don't already have a smart phone; i.e., an iPhone, Android, Blackberry, etc., get one. Period. It is your marketing center away from your computer. Through your smart phone and its various apps, and

---

1 BDCWB has been revived, but all orginal content from the original site is gone forever.

for $30/month, you have unlimited internet. Email, Facebook, Twitter, Blogging....everything at your fingertips. You can keep up with comments on your blog, Facebook status, Tweets, etc. (Remember: even if you do as I suggest and automate the bulk of your marketing tweets, you still must regularly interact with other Tweets by @replying and RTing. And you can tweet about all sorts of interesting things from your event, including a "follow the hashtag" for your particular event.)

I use an iPhone4s, and I cannot recommend it enough. I live on it, especially when traveling, and now users have a choice between AT&T, Sprint, and Verizon as their provider. It will be the best $200 you ever spend[2].

Alternatively, get an iPad. This can do everything an iPhone can do[3], only it's bigger. It's the perfect blend between an iPhone/iPod Touch and a laptop. Light, portable, efficient, etc. Again, in lieu of (or in addition to) a smart phone, this will be your marketing center on-the-go.

Seriously. It's time. Get a smart phone and write it off as a business expense, because this is your mobile office with access to your social networks and marketing hub, your blog.

NEWSLETTERS

Newsletters are a wonderful way to keep in touch with your readership. Have a sign-up sheet on your table at events and have a button on your blog where they can join. Don't send newsletters out often, once a month is the most. Quarterly is plenty. This is just a way to keep in touch and nudge your readers every so often, reminding them of who you are and about your books or upcoming sequel.

Then, during huge marketing pushes, like for a release and blog tour, you have your network ready to inform. Use Newsletters to offer specials to your most loyal fans, like getting a copy of the sequel before the street release date or offering a special discount.

You can also use newsletters as a way to disperse your short fiction, keeping your readers entertained between novels.

TIP: Try Vertial Response for newsletters. Only $0.01 per email. Better than $30/mo contracts while you're still building your readership.

2 $200 for an iPhone5. The iPhone 4s is down to $99, and you can get the iPhone4 for free with contract.
3 Except make phone calls. Plus, it must have a WiFi connection unless you get it 3G enabled.

SHORT STORIES

Some experts have said that the Kindle and other eBook readers will resurrect the short story, and I think they have. But then, perhaps the short story was never dead.

I taught Composition II: Analyzing Short Fiction at Austin Community College for four years, and I only resigned because I moved back to California. I love short stories, but as of 2010, I hadn't written one in years. Mostly because, as every publishing professional will tell you, there is no market for short stories.

They are so very wrong.

I've learned that about these "publishing professionals." There is a market for short stories. There are hundreds of markets for short stories. What they mean is that there is no money in short stories. An agent isn't going to make anything for a short story. Pro-payment for short fiction is $0.05/word. For a 3,500-word short story, that's $175. 15% of $175 is $26.25. No wonder they say there is no market.

But there are, indeed, markets for short stories. Paying and non-paying markets. The paying markets are divided into three categories:

- Pro-payment = $0.05/word or more
- Semi-pro payment = $0.01-0.04/word
- Token payment, usually something like $5-50, depending on the market

So, okay, short stories aren't going to make us rich, but I hope you understand by now that there isn't money in publishing, period. If you're doing this for the money, you're going to be sorely disappointed unless you're that one-in-a-million anomaly like E. L. James (*50 Shades of Grey*), and she made it on a fluke. Seriously. She didn't do it for the money. She wrote fan fiction because she found it fun.

If you're doing this for money, you will be very, very unhappy, indeed.

Do it because you love it.

Do it because you hate it.

Do it because you have to.

Learn your craft. Improve your prose. Have fun.

Short stories don't make money, but they do get you new readers. They do get you exposure, and they do get you credibility as an author.

Plus, they make you a better writer.

Since 2010, I've written over two dozen short stories during a difficult personal time where I couldn't focus on a full-length novel. Between writing these stories and writing my blog 3+ times a week, I have become a better writer. I've become a better-known writer, too.

Short stories. Podcasts. Blog posts. Social networking.

That is a recipe for success.

A short story is between 1,500 and 10,000 words. Over 10,000 words is a novella (10,000-50,000). Less than 1,500 is flash fiction, another fun writing exercise. Chuck Wendig[1], an author who does blogging so very right, offers a flash fiction challenge each week. Try it out.

On a good day, I can write 5,000-8,000 words when I'm in the zone[2] and on a roll. I can easily write a short story in a day. I've written several in a day. However, it takes several days, if not weeks, of "prewriting" before I get to the keyboard. My goal for 2013 is to write one short story a month, and so far I'm on schedule. I wrote one in January called "For the Love of a Book," and it's already been published in *We Love NY: A Romance Anthology to Raise Funds For Hurrican Sandy Relief.* I also wrote one in February called "Come to Me" and another in March called "A Clockwork Heart," both for *Penumbra*, a themed, pro-paying market that is on my "Really Awesome" list, explained momentarily. Since August 2010, I've written 22 short stories, and I will have at least 10 more by the end of the year.

I've had a lot of success with short stories. I've had them podcasted, published in anthologies, in eZines, and directly to Kindle/eBook. I've given them away for free. I've offered them as incentives for a Kickstarter Campaign; mine and those for my colleagues. Many people want to star in their own short story! It's a great incentive to donate to a good cause or a talented artist via Kickstarter or IndieGoGo. In fact, both the stories mentioned above were from such incentives. The contributors get a story starring them, and I get inspiration for a story. They get a copy of the story for themselves, and I get to market it for my career. Win-Win!

---

1 http://terribleminds.com
2 "in the zone" = chocolate, classical music, and coffee, everything I need to write distraction-free

Short stories enable you to experiement with writing styles and story telling techniques. You can toy with voice, POV, tense. Work on your dialogue or endings. Improve your prose. All without commiting to an 85,000-word novel.

I once had the great fortune of being in a writing critique group with Steven Brust, and he told me that a writer has one or two "freebies," the rest we have to work on, develop, and hone. For example, I'm naturally good with dialogue and character development. Emotional storytelling. But I'm not good at endings, multiple-person scenes with more than two people, and my prose is far from the inspired examples set by Kurt Vonnegut or Margaret Atwood. Through writing short stories, I've been able to become more settled in my voice, to trust myself and my instincts, to remember that it's a process. IT'S A PROCESS. The title will come. The ending will come. The conflict will come. Just work the process.

Then, when you've finished your short story, get them edited and beta read[1], and then get them out there. Submit them to a magazine, anthology, or publish them on your blog to give readers a taste of your writing. Or, do all three! Get them out and keep them out until they're published. Many markets will publish reprints. Many won't.

Another option is to publish them straight to Amazon's Amazing Kindle. The Kindle (I'm a huge fan, as I have one myself and rarely read anything in any other format) and other such eReaders have breathed fresh life into the short story.

Amazon has over 18,000 short stories available for the Kindle under Fiction>Short Stories, as well as their featured short stories under Kindle Singles. If you haven't yet gotten your Kindle—now is a great time as they're priced lower than ever and have so many choices in size and color. I have a Kindle 2, but I'm LOVING the PaperWhite[2]! (Hint! Hint!) -- You can find me at Christine Rose[3] on Amazon and just send it as a gift.

Here's a link to my WISH LIST, just in case: http://goo.gl/4Hd9J

---

1 Beta readers are a few people you trust to read your manuscript and give respectful, brutal feedback. They're hard to find, so keep them close when you do.

2 http://goo.gl/eVZU2

3 http://amzn.to/aiGr6Q

DUOTROPE - GET IT NOW

Check out Duotrope.com; it's no longer free to register because too many authors were taking advantage of the free service without donating the suggested $10. Now it costs $50 to register, and it's worth every penny.

Duotrope lists virtually every market for short stories and provides a handy submission tracking device. I truly can't recommend Duotrope highly enough. You can research markets by genre, pay, story length, and more. As you research, you can save particular markets to your favorites list if they stand out or you could add them to your ignore list if they are something you'd never do, like religious fiction, for example.

Their Calendar is a huge source of inspiration. It's a place where themed journal issues and anthologies are chronicled by deadline. You can even filter the Calendar by pay level (any, token, semi, or pro), type (fiction, nonfiction, or poetry), genre, and medium (print, audio, or online).

Here is an example of what the Calendar looks like filtered for pro-payment for February and March 2013 deadlines:

Theme & Deadline Calendar

Calendar of upcoming deadlines for publications, contests, and issues that are themed. Check the publisher's guidelines for full details before submitting.
Subscribe to this information using our RSS feeds: All Upcoming Deadlines | Upcoming Fiction Deadlines | Upcoming Poetry Deadlines | Upcoming Non-Fiction Deadlines

Filter Themes & Deadlines

Type: Fiction	Min. Pay: Pro
Any Genre	Any Medium
Include deadlines with associated fees	Include unthemed deadlines
Filter	

35 deadlines found.

PUBLICATION	THEME	DEADLINE	DAYS TIL	★	
Faces Magazine	The Weird and the Wild	25 Feb 13	8		Track
Crossed Genres Publications: Crossed Genres Magazine	She	28 Feb 13	11		Track
Musa Publishing: Penumbra	Ocean	28 Feb 13	11		Track
Pockets	Everyday Heroes	01 Mar 13	12		Track
New Moon Girls Magazine	Our Favorite Places	01 Mar 13	12		Track
Faces Magazine	The Czech Republic	25 Mar 13	36		Track
Musa Publishing: Penumbra	HG Wells	30 Mar 13	41		Track
Writers	Horror	31 Mar 13	42		Track
Crossed Genres Publications: Crossed Genres Magazine	Expectations	31 Mar 13	42		Track
Pockets	Living Simply	01 Apr 13	43		Track
Tin House	Wild	15 Apr 13	57		Track

Each market is listed on the left along with the theme and deadline. Just a click takes you to that market's page where you can find what they're looking for, submission guidelines, response times, etc. There will be a direct link to their website, which you absolutely must follow and read their submission guidelines, at least. Whether you're finding a market from the Calendar or through your own search, go to the market's website.

Please.

Read their submission guidelines. Follow them TO THE LETTER.

If they say no italics, underline, then ensure your manuscript reflects that. If they say no cover letter, don't send one. If they say they want it in Courier font rather than Times. Make it happen.

Most of them will want your short story formatted in Standard Story Format. Google it, then, do it. It's not rocket science. Follow the rules. Don't give them a reason to reject your story before they even read it.

You'll get enough rejections on your own.

As for cover letters, *KISS*.

This is all it has to say:

Dear Editor,

Please consider my 3600-word Steampunk short story "Of Aether and Aeon" for publication.

Thank you for your consideration.

O. M. Grey
steampunkgrey@gmail.com

If they ask for a short bio, send one. Copy/paste from what you've written during the previous exercise. If they ask for publication credits, send them, but keep it short. Your story will speak for itself.

Short stores are a great way to break into the business of publishing. You can write them relatively quickly, compared to a novel, and you can use them to work on your weaknesses as a writer and truly hone your craft without investing a year of your life. Besides, who knows, you might even attract an agent or a publisher through this method.

You will get lots and lots of rejections. Have I mentioned? Instead of feeling disappointed or rejected, look at it as one less place you have to try. Be happy you got a response! Sometimes, they just leave you hanging for months, or forever. When you get a rejection, update your submission tracker in Duotrope. Then submit it to the next market on your list, following their specific submission guidelines, which might be different from the last.

Don't ever respond to a rejection letter. The only exception to this rule is when the editor sent you a very personal rejection with notes on how to improve your story, which almost never happens. In this instance, just a simple "Thank you for your time and advice" will suffice.

Don't argue. Don't rage. Don't tell them that they just passed up on the next Great American Novelist. Please.

Just don't.

GETTING THE MOST OUT OF DUOTROPE

Especially now that it's no longer free, take some time to get the most out of Duotrope by doing your research and being organized.

Although they have their handy dandy submission tracker, which is invaluable, keep another record for yourself that's more accessible. I use a Moleskine journal. We writers love our fancy journals, so use one to track your own submissions.

Save the first page of the journal for your Dream Lists, explained shortly. Put the title of a short story at the top of each page along with its word count and genre. If you also write poetry, start a poetry section about halfway through, marking the page with a paper clip. List the title of your poem at the top of each page along with line count and type of poetry (rhyming, lyrical, blank verse, etc.).

Near the top, write the word "Submissions," then write the word "Published" a few lines up from the bottom, as you'll have so many more submissions than publications. As you submit, list the date of submission and market. Indicate whether or not the market allows simultaneous submissions, i. e. submitting the story to more than one market at a time. When you get a response, note it in your Duotrope journal with the date of the response.

Update your submission tracker on Duotrope as well.

When you get an acceptance, and after the contract is signed (there should ALWAYS be a contract, even if there is no payment), fill in the first line under "Published."

Like this:

I use tiny post-it notes to remind me where to submit next in case of a rejection. This way, you can do all your research at once because it is rather time consuming.

Let's say I was researching where next to send "Final Word," the story depicted in the photo. It's short at just 2,100 words and has a more literary slant than, say, "Hannah & Gabriel," which is a Steampunk retelling of "Hansel and Gretel," or "A Kiss in the Rain," which is Gothic Paranormal Erotica. Those are both also considerably longer stories. In looking for markets to submit "Final Word," I come across a market that likes retellings of fairy tales. Instead of leaving it to chance (and the extra time it would take) of finding this market again among the thousands Duotrope catalogs, I write that market down on the "Hannah & Gabriel" page's post-it note.

Saves time. Saves frustration.

Keeps you organized.

Remember, this journal is for your benefit. It doesn't replace the Duotrope submission tracker. It works along with it. This way you can have quick reference to which stories are out and which need to go out. After all, once you have a dozen short stories, that submission tracker can get very confusing. In fact, I filter my submission tracker to only show my accepted stories and those awaiting response. Anything rejected gets hidden for the sake of my sanity, not for my ego. This way the submission tracker is streamlined and manageable. I see all my rejections in my notebook, so as not to submit to the same market twice.

Your submission tracker (photo on next page) shows what story you submitted where and when. It also has symbols that indicate whether or not the market accepts simultaneous submissions or not. The numbers on the right are, from left to right, the number of days out, average days to respond for that market, maximum response time for that market, and the number of days when you should expect a response. If that last number goes into the negatives, it's time to query about your story, or in extreme cases, like if it's been over six months, withdraw it.

These numbers are why it's so important to report your submissions, responses, and acceptances/rejections.

On the far right, a link "Update" takes you to the page where you can report that response and make any notes for yourself.

Truly, Duotrope is an invaluable service, well worth the $50. Invest in yourself and in your career.

PIECE	MARKET			DATE SENT	DATE REC'D	RESPONSE	DAYS OUT	AVG RT	EST RT	ETA	
If I Had Known	Long Story Short			31 Mar 2011	31 Mar 2011	Acceptance	0	12	60		Update
Dead Mule Crossing	How the West Was Wicked Anthology closed			31 Mar 2011	02 Apr 2011	Acceptance	2		90		Update
Twenty Mintues	SNM Horror Magazine			20 Jun 2011	27 Jun 2011	Acceptance	7	17	30		Update
The Tragic Tale of Doctor Fausset	Stories in the Ether closed			19 Oct 2011	25 Oct 2011	Acceptance	6				Update
Lost and Found	Tales of the Talisman closed			01 Jul 2012	02 Jul 2012	Acceptance	1	7	45		Update
Look into my Eyes	SNM Horror Magazine			01 Jul 2012	05 Jul 2012	Acceptance	4		30		Update
Railroaded	He Loves Me, He Loves Me Not closed			16 Sep 2012	21 Sep 2012	Acceptance	5				Update
Love is for the Living	Bellows of the Bone Box closed			16 Sep 2012	06 Oct 2012	Acceptance	20				Update
New York Rain	Rusty Nail, The closed			18 Sep 2012	25 Sep 2012	Acceptance	7	9	14		Update
Final Word	Rusty Nail, The closed			18 Sep 2012	25 Sep 2012	Acceptance	7	12	14		Update
Dead Mule Crossing	eSteampunk closed			18 Sep 2012	25 Sep 2012	Acceptance	7				Update
Of Aether and Aeon	After Ever After			08 Jan 2013		Pending Response	40	29		-11	Update
A Tall Order	Bust Fiction			08 Jan 2013		Pending Response	40	80	60	20-40	Update
A Kiss in the Rain	SNM Horror Magazine			08 Jan 2013	26 Jan 2013	Acceptance	18	17	30		Update
Fade of the Innocent	Tor.com			10 Jan 2013		Pending Response	38	254	270	216-232	Update
Missed Connections	TM Magazine			10 Jan 2013		Pending Response	38	49	30	7-11	Update
Twenty Mintues	Nightfall Magazine closed			10 Jan 2013		Pending Response	38	49		11	Update
A Moment of Courage	Survivor Anthology, The closed			11 Jan 2013		Pending Response	37				Update
Look into my Eyes	Survivor Anthology, The closed			11 Jan 2013		Pending Response	37				Update
My Heart Still Wants to Believe	Survivor Anthology, The closed			11 Jan 2013		Pending Response	37				Update
Then, I Cry	Survivor Anthology, The closed			11 Jan 2013		Pending Response	37				Update
Look into my Eyes	Sirens Call eZine			17 Jan 2013	09 Feb 2013	Acceptance	17				Update
Twenty Mintues	Sirens Call eZine			17 Jan 2013	03 Feb 2013	Acceptance	17				Update
A Tall Order	GrantSmb Journal			09 Feb 2013		Pending Response	8	165	150	142-157	Update
The Tragic Tale of Doctor Fausset	Silverthought Online			09 Feb 2013		Pending Response	8	103	90	82-95	Update
Of Aether and Aeon	Allegory			09 Feb 2013		Pending Response	8	46	45	37-38	Update

DREAM LISTS

This little tidbit was given to me by Adrienne Crezo[1] (she's all kinds of awesome), writer and blogger. Make a three-tiered list as you research markets through Duotrope: Dream List, Really Awesome, Wow, That's Cool. On the top tier, Dream List, write down all your highest short story goals. These would probably be professionally paying markets or at least highly coveted markets. It will be different for everyone, depending on the type of short stories and personal preferences. This is my **Dream List** in no particular order except, of course, the first one:

1. New Yorker Magazine
2. Glimmertrain
3. Tin House
4. The Collagist
5. Alask Quarterly Review
6. Zoetrope: All Story
7. The Paris Review
8. Tor
9. Cincinnatti Review
10. The Three Penny Review

---

1 http://www.adriennecrezo.com/ - @a_crezo

11. Asimov's Science Fiction Magazine
12. Lightspeed
13. Ninth Letter
14. Magazine of Fantasy & Science Fiction
15. TriQuarterly

After being published in so many different places and gathering not only some confidence in my writing but also experience in querying and being rejected (AND HOW!), I'm starting to tailor my stories for specific markets. I've submitted to one or two of these, and have been promptly rejected, but I haven't yet submitted a tailored story to them. I have just submitted a story to one in my "Really Awesome" list, below, which was promptly rejected. I first purchased a copy of the magazine and read every short story in there to get a feel of the magazine. Before I submit to any of the above again, I will do the same. I'll get a feel for the magazine, brainstorm, then write a story specifically for that market. If rejected, I'll submit somewhere else, moving down the "Really Awesome" and "Wow, That's Cool" lists first before going elsewhere.

Get them out. Keep them out—until published. Then, get them out there again. Remember, a lot of places will print reprints. It can only help you find your audience and build your author brand: YOUR NAME.

My **Really Awesome** list, again, in no particular order:
1. Nightmare Magazines
2. Clarkesworld
3. Beneath Ceaseless Skies
4. Strange Horizons
5. Penumbra
6. Shimmer
7. Apex
8. Clockwork Phoenix: Tales of Beauty and Strangeness
9. subTerrain Magazine
10. Cosmos
11. Boston Review
12. Black Warrior Review

I recently submitted "Come To Me" to *Penumbra*, and although they rejected it a few days later, it's a good little story. Since it won't appear in *Penumbra*, it will be published elsewhere because I will keep it out there until it is. My short story "Final Word" was just published by *The Rusty Nail*. I wrote it in 2011 and it appeared in my own book *Caught in the Cogs: An Eclectic Collection* but nowhere else since. It took two years, but I kept it out there until it fit somewhere. I was rather pleased it got into *The Rusty Nail,* along with my poem "New York Rain." Quite proud. I'm moving up, one step at a time.

Get them out. Keep them out. Until published.

Write more.

My **Wow, That's Cool!** list:

1. The Pedestal Magazine
2. SteamPunk Magazine
3. Buzzy Mag
4. Wily Writers
5. Podcastle
6. Leodegraunce
7. Enchanted Conversations: A Fairy Tale Magazine
8. Absinthe Revival
9. Stupefying Stories
10. Flash Fiction Online

Once you get your story published, PROMOTE IT! Tell everyone! Blast out newsletters. Blog about it. Facebook. Twitter. Goodreads. Create a Facebook Event celebrating it.

I was astounded when one of my editors told me that most authors don't promote their work after publication. Wherever your story appears, in print or online, to purchase or for free, let everyone know about it.

Truly, short stories are a great way to both improve your skill and find new readers. I've found it as invaluable as any social networking tool for marketing. Build your career, hone your craft, and find new readers all at once.

PART III:
EBOOKS & AMAZON

There are currently 180 eBooks for every 100 hardcovers[1] being released. And that number is steadily growing. This is nearly two to one. Jeff Bezos, CEO of Amazon.com, said in a *USA Today* article[2]: "we will surpass paperback sales in the next nine to 12 months." eBooks are definitely the wave of the future, and the future is here. Now. Through eBook sales, self-publishers have literally become millionaires. Names like Amanda Hocking and J. A. Konrath are almost as well known as Stephanie Meyer and Stephen King in literary circles.

This is an exciting time to be an emerging author, as there are so many options for publishing your book and getting the word out to your potential market. The old system is dying. The power is being taken out of the hands of the media and distributors and publishers. Readers and authors are gaining more control over what is published and what is discovered. Much of this has to do with the eBook revolution.

It all has to do with the internet.

THE EBOOK REVOLUTION

Borders is bankrupt.[3] Barnes & Noble is up for sale. Amazon is showing record sales, especially in eBooks, and has become one of the Big Boys as a publisher as well. I've heard again and again how authors

---

1 Miller, Carrie Cain. "E-books Top Hardcovers at Amazon." New York Times. 19 Jul 2010. Web. 07 Apr. 2011.

2 Baig, Edward C. "Volume of Kindle book sales stuns Amazon's Jeff Bozos." USA Today. 29 July 2010. Web. 03 Apr. 2011.

3 Spector, Mike and Jeffrey A. Trachtenberg. "Chapter 11 for Borders, New Chapter for Books." The Wall Street Journal. February 12, 2011. Web.

are seeing greater sales from their eBooks than from their paperbacks. We've experienced it ourselves. We sell between 5x - 60x as many eBooks (mostly on Kindle) than we do in paperback.

Why?

The price point + the convenience = The Impulse Buy.

Independent authors understand what the NYBB have yet to figure out: a lower price point means more sales. More sales = more money, even at the lower rate. Don't be like the NYBB who price their eBooks over $6.00, some I've seen as high as $15.99.

This is ridiculous.

What they don't seem to comprehend is that it doesn't matter that they have a huge overhead regardless of whether the book is in print or in electronic format. What matters is the consumer's perception, and a consumer is not going to buy an eBook for $8.99 when they can buy the print book for $8.99. They're especially not going to buy an eBook for $8.99 by an unknown author from a NYBB when they can buy three eBooks for the same amount of money from independent publishers and authors. Because, guess what, very few people look to see who the publisher is when shopping on Amazon. They look at the author's name, the book cover, the blurb, and the reviews. If they are only going to risk $2.99, they'll give a new author a try, especially if they liked the free sample download.

eBooks are leveling the playing field between NYBBs are independent authors. Same distribution. Same level of visibility, more or less.

Now the market will decide what to read. Newspapers won't tell them what to read. Purchased real estate on bookstore kiosks won't tell them what to read. Word of Mouth, browsing, and sample downloads will help readers decide what to buy.

Hopefully eBooks will help minimize the disgusting amount of waste produced from over-zealous print runs and the antiquated bookstore return policy.

eBooks are the future, and the sales reflect this.

"eBooks, iPhone, uKnow?"

More and more books are available in electronic formats. I, for one, am very happy about this!

My husband and I are long-standing environmentalists, and anything that will reduce the miserable waste of paper in this country is okay with me.

Sure, there are things that must be printed. Granted.

Just think of the junk mail that STILL comes in your mail.

Think of the newspaper that's delivered to many households every day. Where one or two pages (at most) are read by the average newspaper subscriber. The other 45 line the bottom of a bird cage or get thrown directly in the trash (or hopefully the recycling bin).

Think of the magazines you never have time to read.

Think of the pile of romance novels and mysteries and others you find at your local book reseller. And those are just a fraction of the ones that were thrown away.

Perhaps eBooks will help reduce the amount of paper used. Newspapers just need to go online with their news and deliver their product electronically. Magazines, too. The information is still there!

With things like the Kindle and even the iPhone, it's easier than ever to take your library with you and download the latest news right to your palm. The iPhone has several sources for book downloads. The iPhone even has a Kindle Application!

Brilliant.

The eBook will not replace the printed book, of course. Never. Not in our lifetimes. Just as email SPAM hasn't replaced Junk Mail. It's just reduced it.

Although, I'm not sure the iPhone is the greatest device on which to read an entire book. At least not for me, but there are many people who read books on their iPhone. Some have even read our book on the iPhone! And many more have read it on the Kindle.

But still, the majority of readers have read our book in paperback form.

As my husband said yesterday, "It doesn't matter how you enjoy it, just as long as you enjoy it." Download a few chapters for free. (The Kindle always allows a free download of the first chapter.) If you like it, then buy the book. Saves time, trees, and money!

(First published on C&E blog[1], March 9, 2009)

Up until the eBook revolution, one of the biggest reasons self-publishing has held its stigma for so long is the issue of quality. As previously mentioned, self-publishing conjures up images of poor writing, amateur layout, and badly photoshopped covers, something that truly needs to stop. There are so many talented artists in need of work, and they can create a beautiful cover for little money.

There is no excuse for an amateur cover.

But now with eBooks, readers can download a sample of the book. If the first chapter is riddled with errors, shoddy writing, and bad grammar, they move onto the next one. There are, after all, plenty of books available. Remember, 950 books are published every day, and that figure is printed books.

Publishers are scrambling to catch up. They've been working on the same old tired business model for so long, they don't know what to do with all this new technology. Now that the Kindle can actually read to you, in a very computer-generated sounding voice, many publishers are screaming that it will hurt their audiobook sales.

---

1 http://www.christineandethanrose.com/blog

"Kindle Swindle"

In honor of eBook Week (Mar 8-14), we'll be focusing our posts on eBooks! (imagine that!)

I recently read an article in the Dallas Morning News calling for Kindle to pay audio rights for the books it reads aloud. Roy Blount Jr, who authored the piece, makes some valid points but leaves me unconvinced. As he is the president of the Authors Guild, I can understand his concern. But as an author myself, I can see a greater benefit from not pursuing audio rights for eBooks.

Blount's argument is that audio rights are more valuable than eBook rights. This is true, but if eBooks can be read audibly, this can only increase the value of eBooks and the rights to them. This seems like a win-win situation to me. Everyone who listens to an eBook has paid for the right to experience the book. Does it really matter what form they choose?

As for the Kindle taking the place of a parent at bedtime, the ones who really lose out are the parents and child who lose a shared experience, and I truly can't foresee the Kindle taking the place of any loving parent (no more than it will take the place of a printed book).

Audio books are also expensive to produce, while eBooks cost almost nothing. Why not pass some of that savings on to the consumer? I also can't imagine that a computer generated voice will replace professional entertainers anytime soon. I have often chosen to listen to a particular book because I liked the narrator, but by the same token I have abandoned listening to books I was really interested in because the narrator disagreed with me.

My book *Rowan of the Wood* is available for download on Kindle, and I have no problem with it being read aloud by person or machine. However someone chooses to enjoy it is fine by me, as long as they enjoy it.

(First published on C&E blog[1] March 8, 2009 - by Ethan Rose.)

On top of the audiobook issue, there is the ongoing debate over DRM, Digital Rights Management. This term is used to describe the technology that supposedly controls copyright and piracy. If you choose to protect your eBook by engaging the DRM, it shouldn't be pirated. But for me and Neil Gaiman, we say: Steal My Book! (Watch "Gaiman on Copyright Piracy and the Web[2]" on YouTube). In 2012, Tor announced they were launching a DRM-free digital bookstore[3]. Yep. It's going away.

By allowing readers to openly share your work if they so choose, your work will be more widespread. You have the opportunity to "go viral" much more easily if readers can share your work. You want people reading your work. You want people talking about your work. You want this, and trust me, you aren't losing any sales.

Still, this is a huge controversy.

> *The more people read your work,*
> *the more will love your books.*

Remember Marketing Maxim #4: It's a number's game.

Get it out there any way possible. They will remember your name and read the next thing you put out, and they will spend the $2.99 for an eBook the next time. If you get enough readers, you could find yourself in a situation similar to Ms. Hocking:

1 http://www.christineandethanrose.com/blog
2 OpenRightsGroup. "Gaiman on Copyright Piracy and the Web." YouTube. 03 Feb. 2011. Web. 03 Apr. 2011.
3 Owen, Laura Hazard. "Five digital lessons from BookExpo America 2012." paidContent. 8 June 2012. Web. 18 Feb. 2013.

"Self-Publishing's Golden Goose"

If you pay attention to the publishing world at all, then you have heard the name Amanda Hocking. You likely have also heard the name J. A. Konrath. They are currently the greatest self-publishing success stories circulating cyberspace, but others are not far behind.

Amanda Hocking is 26-years-old and lives in Minnesota. She has already written and published nine books. She started self-publishing them via Amazon's Kindle last year, and she has sold over 900,000 copies of those nine books, hitting the USA today bestseller list. Seriously.

Last week, New York was knocking on her door. Quite loudly, it seemed. The Big Boys fought a week-long bidding war for the rights of her books. The bid went, as reported by The Times[4] last week, was into the millions. On Thursday, she signed a four-book deal with St. Martins for over two million dollars.[5] Nice.

Amanda talks about her decision on her blog.[6] Very interesting read.

On the flip side, J. A. Konrath started publishing the traditional way with a NYBB. But, as he had piles of manuscripts that NY didn't want, and as the rights of his published books were slowly reverting back to him after having gone out of print, he decided to self-publish via Amazon's Kindle, too.

Now he makes a healthy six-figures a year as well. And he is not quiet about it or his growing aversion to traditional publishing. He trumpets his success and some of his colleagues' successes on his blog: *A Newbie's Guide to Publishing*. In fact, he

---

4 Bosman, Julie. "Noted Self-Publisher May Be Close to a Book Deal." The New York Times. 21 Mar. 2011. Web. 04 Apr. 2011.

5 Bosman, Julie. "A Successful Self-Publishing Author Decides to Try the Traditional Route." The New York Times. 24 Mar. 2011. Web. 5 Apr. 2011.

6 http://amandahocking.blogspot.com/

has written so much about the topic, including how and why he did it himself, that he now has a Kindle book out by the same name. 350,000 words from his blog on how he turned orphaned manuscripts into a fine living…and had more time to write.

Sounds like every writer's dream: to make a good living through your craft and have enough time to keep writing.

Authors across Twitter, Facebook, and the rest of cyberspace are seeing dollar signs. They want a piece of this action, and who can blame them? But as independent authors, you must take the time (and the money) to create a quality product. This means to *hire* someone to make your book cover. Don't even attempt to do it yourself unless you are a professional graphic designer. Seriously. This means to *hire* someone to edit and proofread your book. You cannot effectively edit your own work.

Even if you do all this, will every self-published author see numbers like these? Unlikely. Just as there are rock stars in traditional publishing, there are rock stars in self-publishing. But I think writers can learn a lot from these models. There are more ways to get your work published than ever before, and self-publishing is becoming more and more viable (and socially acceptable) every day.

New York doesn't know what to do. Out of one side of their mouth they say they won't touch it because it's been self-published. Through the other side they're offering millions to a self-published author. But this is par for New York Publishing. They change their mind as often as a stoned frat boy changes channels.

No doubt, however, that with the growing popularity of eBooks, self-published and independent authors have a better chance than ever to be seen and to find a readership. With some luck and marketing, they might even be able to scrape a living together. Then if they attract a NYBB in the mean time, they have options and they can get a decent contract on their own terms.

The time of the author is returning.

(First published 28 March 2011 on my blog[1])

AMAZON, SMASHWORDS, & PUBIT!

AMAZON IS AN AUTHOR'S BEST FRIEND

Hands down.

I get a check from Amazon every month. In fact, I get four, sometimes five: two from Kindle sales (both US and EU), one from CreateSpace sales, one from Amazon Associates, and sometimes one from Seller Central (which I use to sell my documentaries).

Granted, I'm not paying my mortgage with those checks. Yet. But often it is enough to cover one of the car payments. Other authors are not only paying their mortgage, they're making a sweet living on just Kindle sales. J. A. Konrath makes a six-figure income from his Kindle sales alone.

Konrath is Amazon's golden boy. Because of his extensive posts about the benefits of self-publishing and his success on the Kindle, Amazon has partnered up with him, which has only made him more successful. Now his books often appear on the Amazon home page, etc. In exchange, he now promotes Amazon's CreateSpace for print books, which now is my top recommendation for the emerging author, as I mentioned before.

Unless you lost your eBook publishing rights to an Independent Press or a NYBB, you can maximize your exposure and profits by making your books available on Amazon's Kindle.

Never give your eBook rights away for free. Get *something* for them.

---

1 http://christinerose.wordpress.com

To maximize your earnings with Amazon and to get your books available on the Kindle, the first thing you'll need is an account with Amazon. It's free to set up, and you likely already have one if you buy anything from Amazon at all. If you don't have an account, there is a link at the top of every Amazon.com page that reads "New customer? Start here."

Start there.

You will only need your email address, name, and password. Once you've created an account with Amazon.com, you are ready to become an Amazon Author, complete with your own author page and sales figures; an Amazon Associate, where you will earn a few pennies from every sale you lead to Amazon; an Amazon Seller, where you can sell used books and other items, your own books, if you don't choose to be distributed via CreateSpace or Lightning Source[1], and many other things. In addition to all this, you will set up as a Kindle Direct Publisher (formerly Digital Text Platform, DTP).

The most important of these for authors is the Kindle Direct Publisher (KDP), so let's begin there.

SETTING UP YOUR KDP ACCOUNT

At the very bottom, in the footer of any Amazon page, there are several links under the orange heading "Make Money with Us."

- Click on "See all."
- Scroll down to the "Independent-Publishing" section on the bottom left. On the right, note the "Affiliate Program," we'll be coving that shorly.
- Under "Kindle Books," click "Learn More."
- On the next page, click "Get Started."
- Crazy, but you might have to sign in again. They do this often to avoid fraud and check for your password.
- Read and accept the KDP Terms of Service. Click "Agree."

---

1 Another choice is Amazon Advantage. Amazon will order straight from you, but LSI is still the best. Amazon Advantage can turn into a huge hassle, as they order just a few copies at a time. They might order three books today, and then another three two days later. Shipping becomes tedious and expensive. With CreateSpace, it's just so not worth it anymore.

- You're done! Almost. You are now looking at an empty bookshelf and a button that says "Add a new title." This is where you will upload your Kindle books in the future, so bookmark this page.
- Notice a gold box at the top right that says "Your account information is incomplete."
- And, yes, you'll have to sign in again. It's a hassle, but it's safe because we are now dealing with money.
- Under "Your Account," fill in your business name (if you're selling as a single author, then use your name. If you've created an LLC publishing company, use that name.)
- Add your address, tax information (SSN if sole proprietor and EIN if General Partnership or LLC), and, very important, your bank information. Amazon will direct deposit funds into your checking account. Or, of course, you can opt to have them send you checks in the mail, but that costs $8 per check. Direct deposit is the way to go.
- Once completed, return your bookshelf by clicking "Bookshelf" near the top of the screen.

ADD A NEW TITLE FOR THE KINDLE

Adding a new title for the Kindle is fairly simple. You will want to have your eBook in MS Word, preferably. When you upload it, the Kindle will convert your .doc or .docx to the Kindle format. This is the simplest way to do it; however, it might not be the best way depending on your book and the complexity level of your formatting. Overall, you will want your eBook to look good on the Kindle. This means you cannot have any strange formatting hidden in the MS Word document. It has to be clean.

There are programs you can buy, and there are even some for free, that will convert your files to every eBook format, including PDF, ePub, html, and others. One of these programs is called Calibre. Another is Sigil[2]. They are free to download, but if you are making money off your eBooks, please consider donating to help keep it free. Or, as happened with Duotrope, they'll have to charge to cover their own costs. The

2 http://calibre-ebook.com; http://code.google.com/p/sigil/

software is available for Windows, Mac OS, and Linux. Author Guido Henkel has an entire blog series[1] about how to effectively format your eBook. If you are technically savvy, this will help you create a beautifully formatted eBook in all formats.

Personally, I only find this necessary for books that have special formatting like numbered series, footnotes, images, etc. If you're uploading an eBook that is only text, the default Kindle converter on the KDP is sufficient. But the formatting on the MS Word document must still be clean so that there aren't any weird hidden characters and such. Since there are so many word processing programs out there, I won't go into exactly how to do that. Programs like Open Office and Mac's Pages from iWork can export into MS Word, and each of those programs have different menus for formatting. Use Google to search how to remove unwanted formatting from your specific program. There will be a step-by-step guide somewhere on the internet for each word processing program.

Under the "Community" link near the top of your KDP dashboard page are several articles on formatting and publishing content to KDP, as well as forums for added user support.

Smashwords, which I'll cover after this Amazon section, has a StyleGuide that really helps you clear the formatting. You can download the PDF at http://www.smashwords.com. You will need to do this for the Smashwords' version anyway.

Once you have a .doc/x with clean formatting, you are ready to upload your first title to KDP and start promoting your Kindle title and making a little extra money. Preview your book after upload to see how it will look on each Kindle. There is even a spell check now that might catch that stray typo missed by your editor. Never know.

You do not need an ISBN to publish on Kindle, but you will need one to publish on Smashwords if you want it in their Premium Distribution. You can use the same ISBN for all eBook formats, as it is the ISBN for the eBook version of your book.

---

1 http://guidohenkel.com/2010/12/take-pride-in-your-ebook-formatting/

STEPS FOR ADDING A NEW TITLE ON KDP

- Click "Add a new title"
- Fill in the title and description section for your eBook. The description is very important, as it will often be the deciding factor on whether or not a reader will buy your book. Use the 100 word blurb you wrote earlier in the Marketing section. Include any review quotes here as well, especially if they are from reputable sources. But even if they are just book reviewing blogs, include them. Three or four work nicely.

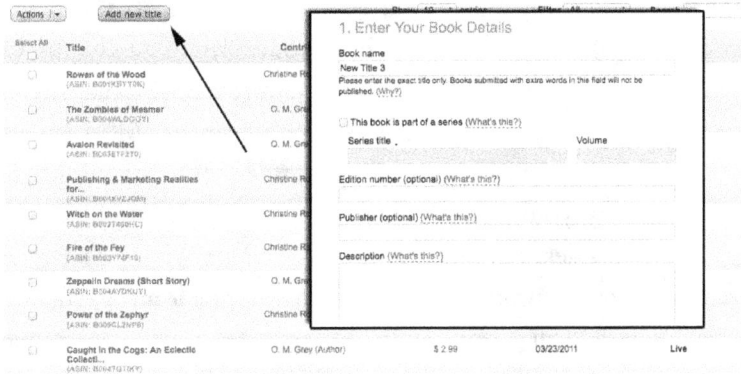

- Fill out the Publishing Details and Publishing Rights. Then you will have to add some keywords so potential readers can find your book in their searches. If any of these are confusing to you, click on the "What's this?" link beside each for more information.
- Now you're ready to upload the Product Image. It must be in RGB, rather than CMYK, for internet viewing. If it's in CMYK, then the colors will go all wonky online. Ask your designer to convert your cover to RGB in Photoshop. It literally takes a minute to do this. Your book cover must look professional, even if you're just releasing the title on eBook. People truly do judge a book by its cover, so make sure it's a nice one.
- As for the Book Content, it's up to you whether or not to enable digital rights management (DRM). It's a very controversial topic.

Enabling DRM helps stop piracy; however, several authors, including Neil Gaiman, as previously mentioned, have claimed that piracy has only helped in their book sales. Ultimately, it's up to you. Once you choose this option, you cannot change your choice. So do some research on the subject if it concerns you. Make Google your new best friend.

- When finished with the above, click on "Save and Continue."
- On the next page, you will set your price and royalties. If you have all the rights to your book, then click Worldwide Rights. This means anyone around the world will be able to download your book. It won't be limited to country.
- Next, set the price. This is also a controversial topic. I've found the perfect price for an eBook (novel length, 50K+) is between $2.99 and $4.99. Novellas (10K-50K) $1.99. Short stories, $0.99. By pricing your book higher than this $2.99, you'll be inhibiting your sales. $2.99 is a great price point for a reader to take a chance on an unknown author. If you price it more, you will get a higher royalty, but you'll sell far fewer books. For sequels or new releases, you can start with $4.99, but drop it down to $2.99 after afew months.
- Choose your royalty option. I go for the 70%, of course. But you can only choose 70% if the price is at least $2.99. For novellas and short stories, you'll have to settle for the 35% royalty option. Even the 35% royalty option is 7x what you'd get from a Big Boy publisher.
- Then choose whether or not you would like your book to participate in the Kindle lending program. This is where a user who has purchased your book can lend it to a friend for two weeks. I recommend you allow this. It ultimately increases your readership. You want people to read your book, even if not every single person pays for it.
- Choose whether or not you would like to be part of KDP Select[1]. Since most of your eBook sales will be on the Kindle anyway,

1 http://kdp.amazon.com/self-publishing/KDPSelect

I'd recommend this for at least 3 months. This means you can't have your title available anywhere else for those three months. However, you will also be allowed 5 promotional days within that 90 days to make your book free. Great for promotional pushes, especially right before another title's release, like the sequel. Give it away. Yes. Do it. You'll get more readers to purchase other/future titles. This also enables Amazon Prime users to read your book for free the entire time it's part of KDP Select. Great selling point. Plus, you get a share of the KDP Select global fund in exchange for this every time someone borrows your book, which in February 2013 was $1.2 million. Win-win.

- Click "Save & Publish," and you've just published your first book on the Kindle. After a few days it will go live on Amazon.

About once a week, check under the "Reports" link near the top of your KDP dashboard to see how many books you're selling.

You will want to set up automated tweets to promote your book daily via TweetAdder, or whatever automated service you chose. And you will want the link to be from your Amazon Associate account.

So, while we're waiting for your Kindle book to go live, let's set up your Associate account.

SETTING UP AN AMAZON ASSOCIATE ACCOUNT

Through Amazon Associates (AA), you can add widgets to your website[2], send links directly to Twitter, and link to any product on Amazon. The brilliance of this is that even if the consumer doesn't buy your book or whatever product you linked to, if they buy anything on Amazon within 24hrs after following your link, you will get a little piece of the pie. And it is a little piece, but depending on your following and marketing skills, it can be a nice little extra something for very little work.

- Go back to Amazon.com and scroll back down to the bottom.
- Click on "Become an Affiliate."

---

2 Free WordPress sites will not display these <iframe> widgets, but you can still create a link to Amazon, just not a fancy one with pretty pictures. Click the "Share" button to post directly to Twitter or Facebook.

- You will need to register a new account for the Associate's program. Use the same email/password you did for your basic Amazon account for ease.
- Strangely, residents of Colorado, North Carolina, and Rhode Island are not eligible to participate in the Associates program.
- Fill our your name, address, and the rest. Click "Next: Your Website Profile."
- Enter the name of your website, if you chose to go with a WordPress blog, this will be your author's name.
- Enter the URL of the website and what your website is about.
- Choose the topics: "Manufacturer/Publisher/Author/Artist" for the first and "Books" for the second, or whichever best describes your website.
- Tick Books, Digital Downloads, and Kindle under the items you intend to list, or whatever else you intend to promote.
- Type of site: Blog.
- Drive traffic: Social Networks and Blogs, and any others that are applicable.
- Make other choices based on your information, tick the "Agree to Terms," then click "Finish."
- At the top of the next page is your unique Associate's ID.
- Click "Specify Payment Method Now" and fill in your tax and banking information. Again, direct deposit is the easiest. You can also choose Amazon.com gift card if you want to turn around and spend your income on Amazon. The balance will go straight into your Amazon account.
- After you complete that information, Amazon will take you to your Associates' dashboard. Here you can see your monthly earnings, download reports from a certain time span, and read more about the Associates Program.
- Click "Get Started Now" in the left sidebar to take a tour on how Associates works and how to start earning money.

- Across the top of every Associates' page are several tabs: Links & Banners, Widgets, aStore, Product Advertising API, Affiliate Programs, and Reports. The tour will show you how each of these work.

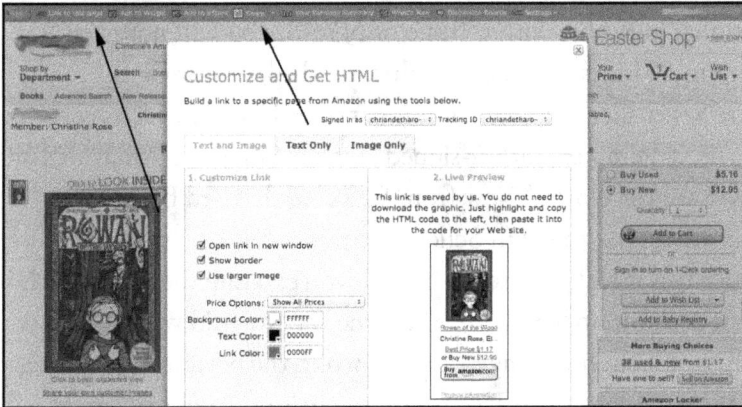

- Go back to Amazon.com. You will now see a gray toolbar across the top of the website with "Link to this page," "Add to Widget," "Share," and more. This will now appear on every Amazon page for ease of sharing.

TIP

Create a .txt file on your desktop with all the AA links saved for easy access. Click on "Link to the Page" then the tab that says "Text Only." Copy the URL between the quotations marks after "href=". Use a URL shortener like tinyurl. com or bit.ly to make the URL manageable, then save it to your .txt file. Do this with every novel, short story, even to your Author Page. Then use those links EVERYWHERE. Email. Blog. Sidebar on your blog. Facebook. Twitter. Every time you mention yourself or your book, add this AA link. These links are directly tied into your AA account. If a customer clicks on this link and buys anything in the next 24 hours, you will get a percentage of that sale.

Brilliant, really.

AMAZON SELLER ACCOUNT

There are two types of Amazon Seller Accounts: Amazon Seller Central and Amazon Advantage. If you set up your paperback/hardback books with Lightning Source or CreateSpace, or if you went through a traditional publisher, either Indie or NYBB, you will not need Amazon Advantage. This is to sell books directly through Amazon.

The Seller Central is what you can use, however. Here you can sell other used items or author-signed books. On most Amazon listings, you will see the words "New from $x.xx" and "Used from $x.xx." These people are selling through Seller Central.

Since this is really a side business, I won't go into the details on how to set that account up here. Start the same way you did with the other two, on Amazon.com homepage, scroll down to the bottom, and underneath the "Make Money with Us" heading, click on "Sell on Amazon." The next page will take you through the ins and outs of each of your choices.

AMAZON AUTHOR CENTRAL

The last important thing to set up on Amazon is your Author Central page. Go to https://authorcentral.amazon.com to get started.

- Click on the "New to Author Central" link and sign into Amazon.
- Accept the terms and conditions, enter your author name. Amazon will search for your books on its site.
- Follow the remaining prompts to complete your account.

Once you've created your account, you can fill out your profile by adding your author bio, your author picture, RSS feed[1] from your blog, and put in book signings or other author events you have scheduled.

One of the many great things about Author Central is that it tracks your sales information. You can see how many copies of your book were purchased through Amazon and where each sale came from by state or country just by clicking the "Sales Info" link on your dashboard's top menu.

---

1 RSS = Real Simple Syndication. This is how one subscribes to various blogs. You will need your RSS URL to link your blog to your Amazon Author Page, Goodreads, and other places. If you don't know how to find your RSS feed, Google it for your specific blog service. Then save the URL somewhere handy.

Under the link "Customer Reviews," you have access to all the reviews for your titles in one place.

The customer service at Amazon is amazing, and the customer service for Author Central is even better. They will either call you within five minutes via phone or answer you query within 24 hours via email. This way, you can stay on top of your titles, ensuring each new anthology containing your short story, Kindle Single, or new novel is visible on your Author Central page. Create an Amazon Associate's link to your Author page and use it wherever you mention yourself on your blog or elsewhere.

Amazon is one of the best friends an emerging author can have. From a few extra dollars to having your work available in the largest worldwide bookstore, Amazon helps independent authors.

TWO WORDS ABOUT AMAZON PRIME

Get it.

It's so worth the $79/yr. That's the same price as a monthly Netflix subscription for streaming video. With Amazon Prime, you get to view lots of Amazon Instant Videos for free, get free 2-day shipping, plus get to borrow Kindle books for free! This will come in very handy when you're reading and reviewing books for your blog content. Remember, when you review these books, use an Amazon Associate's link to encourage people to buy it.

At the very least, do the free 30 day trial.[2]

SMASHWORDS

After you get your book up on the Kindle, it's time for you to make it available for other eBook readers like B&N Nook and the Sony eReader, among others, unless, of course, you chose to be part of the KDP Select program. The easiest way to do this is to go through Smashwords.

At http://www.smashwords.com, you are able to do this with little problem. They, too, have an affiliate program, so sign up for that as well (Become a Smashwords Affiliate link in the top menu).

---

2 http://goo.gl/x5HZF

Smashwords, once you strictly follow their Style Guide, will distribute your books to Apple's iPad (iBookstore, if you have an ISBN), B&N Nook, and many other outlets. Additionally, their servers will convert your eBook to all eBook formats. You will have a page right there on Smashwords to direct your readers, but your books will also appear in the iBookstore and at Barnes & Nobles website.[1] They call this their Premium Distribution Status.

They give a whopping 85% to authors[2], the best yet. You can set your own price, again the best price for a novel is $2.99, and set the percentage of sampling, how much of your book a reader can download for free. They recommend at least 20% sampling. Additionally, you can create promotional coupons to give your readers up to 100% off for a time period that you set. This is a great way to give your book away during a blog tour or other promotional push without having to go back in and change the price.

To start, sign up for an account.

- Go to http://www.smashwords.com and sign up by clicking the word "Join" in the top menu.
- Fill in the pertinent information and you're ready to go.
- Via their dashboard, you can upload your title, book cover, and set your price and sampling. It is also through this dashboard that you can see how many copies have been sampled and/or purchased.

Unlike Amazon's Kindle, you will need an ISBN for your eBook on Smashwords if you want it to be in their Premium Distribution (i.e., available for the iPad and Sony). If you're publishing straight to eBook only, that is not doing a print version of your book at all, you can buy a single ISBN through Smashwords. As mentioned earlier, unless you plan to *just* do this, you should buy at least 10 ISBNs from Bowker

---

1 Alternatively, you can distribute your eBook straight to Barnes & Noble via their PubIt option. Cut out Smashwords as the middle man.

2 85% of what they get. If your reader purchases straight from Smashwords, you get 85%. From another source, like B&N or iBookstore, you get 85% of what Smashwords gets (generally 65-70%).

for the paperback, hardback, eBook, and possibly audiobook[3] of your novel. If you only plan to publish it via Kindle and Smashwords, you don't need to buy these ISBNs. You don't even need an ISBN to publish on Smashwords, but if you want to be in their Premium Distribution program, you will need one. Since most of your eBook sales will be on the Kindle, you might not need an ISBN at all. There are Nook readers out there who will ask about availability for the Nook, which uses the ePub format. If you don't want to mess with an ISBN yet, you can send them to Smashwords to download the ePub from there, or you can create one via Sigil and sell to them direct through PayPal along with a fancy PDF option.

PUBIT!

"PubIt!: Barnes & Noble Plays Catch-up with Amazon's KDP"

At the DFW Writer's Conference in February 2011, I attended a presentation on Barnes & Noble's relatively new PubIt! system. PubIt! (yes, the exclamation point is necessary) is Barnes & Noble's answer to Amazon's Kindle Digital Publishing (KDP) system, an interface that allows authors and small publishers to publish eBook directly to Amazon.com for the Kindle. Now users can publish eBook directly to the B&N Nook via PubIt! without going through an eBook middle man like Smashwords.

The PubIt! interface is very user-friendly and self explanatory as one navigates through it. Users get a straight 65% royalty on sales of eBooks priced between $2.99 and $9.99, a little less than Amazon.com's option of 70%, but not unreasonably so. Books priced below or above those figures earn a straight 40% royalty, a little more than Amazon.com's 35% option, but not significantly so.

---

3 A great way to make an audiobook is to serialize it via podcast, then you'll have all the files to burn and replicate onto CDs.

So, for an eBook priced at $2.99, the author will get $1.94 via PubIt! If they publish through Smashwords at the same price, the author gets $1.79 per eBook sold for the NOOK. One, of course, should still publish through Smashwords for all their other distribution, like Sony, Diesel, Kobo, and most importantly Apple's iBookstore. Just choose to omit Barnes & Noble at Smashwords to publish through PubIt! Get that extra $0.15 per book.

Personally, I think this is great, and it's about time. Barnes & Noble launched PubIt! back in October 2010, but the first I heard of it was at the Writer's Conference in February. Perhaps this is because I have ceased to pay attention to Barnes & Noble online. When deciding whether to get a Kindle or a Nook as an eReader (another thing B&N had to scramble to catch up to Amazon.com), the choice for a Kindle was a no-brainer. They were relatively the same price, and sure, the Nook had a fancy color strip at the bottom (this was before the full color Nook), but when I looked at the pricing of eBooks on the two sites, Barnes & Noble's eBook pricing was almost always higher. In fact, most of their books are priced higher than Amazon.com.

The choice was clearly a Kindle, and I love it.

Barnes & Noble, after all, is a brick-and-mortar book store, and they have held on tight to that image until very recently. When I venture out to a book store, it's almost always to a Barnes & Noble. I worked for Barnes & Noble in grad school. We've signed books at countless Barnes & Nobles across the country, and they've been rather good to us. They would usually give us a free Starbucks to enjoy during our book signing, so what's not to love?

The B&N representative at the conference acted as if B&N came up with this idea all on their very own. The presenter took us step-by-step through the set up process, bashing Amazon whenever he possibly could. But never once did he admit that Amazon has been doing this for a few years, and ultimately does it better. After all, it's all Amazon does. They're not trying to maintain hundreds of huge book superstores across the country, dozens of warehouses, a streamlined online presence, all while staying on the cutting edge of the rapidly changing technology.

Still, B&N is trying to catch up, and I commend them for that. But they have a long way to go.

As an independent author over the past few years, I've become increasingly disenchanted with Barnes & Noble, especially online. Until this latest push with PubIt!, they have not been friendly to the little guy. Certainly not in comparison with Amazon.com. Amazon not only welcomes authors and other small businesses to deal directly through Amazon.com, with their KDP (and now CreateSpace), Seller Accounts, and Amazon Advantage, they also offer authors their own page (Author Central), complete with bios, RSS feeds from their blog, and detailed sales information from BookScan.

Barnes & Noble does none of that.

To top it all off, Amazon has their amazing and easy-to-use Associates Affiliate program, where anyone can make a few pennies off Amazon purchases through a special, easily integrated associates code.

Let me tell you, those pennies add up.

Barnes & Noble has an affiliate program, too; but it is so complicated (and requiring a different site with different log-in credentials) that it's not worth the effort, especially since so many more people shop at Amazon.com.

Although my first choice in brick-and-mortar book stores is still Barnes & Noble (even before Borders' bankruptcy), my online allegiance remains with Amazon.com. They have the best selection, the best prices, and they love authors.

Kudos to Barnes & Noble for entering into the 21st century of book buyers. I hope they continue to evolve with the marketplace. They'll need to if they don't want to follow Borders.

(Post first appeared on The Best Damn Creative Writing Blog, April 11, 2011.)

PUBLISH A BOOK ON PUBIT!

- Go to http://bn.com
- Mouse-over the menu heading NOOKbooks, choose PubIt! Books from the drop-down menu. Or, alternatively, just start at http://pubit.barnesandnoble.com
- In the bottom right corner, sign in with your BN.com account number. If you don't have one, you will need to create one.
- Under the Account Setup screen, enter the Contact Information and the Publisher Information. Click "Continue."
- Accept the Terms & Conditions, you will need to scroll through the entire document before it will let you choose the "I have read and agree..." radio button.
- Fill out your banking information to ensure your sales percentage gets direct-deposited into your account. You must enter Credit Card information for "the unlikely event that you receive more returns than sales."
- Click "Add your first eBook."
- Fill in the books information, upload the .doc for conversion, and upload the cover image (RGB for web). Cover image must be between 750 and 2000 pixels.
- Once you upload the book interior, a really cool virtual NOOK appears for the preview. Ensure it looks good.

- Fill out the information in part 4. "Help Readers Find Your eBook." You do not need an ISBN, similar to the Kindle, but if you have one (you'll need it for iBookstore, etc.) use it here. Fill out the series, pages (if applicable), and other information in this section.
- Part 5: enter your subject categories, keywords, descriptions of the book & author, and any editorial reviews.
- SAVE. Always save.
- Choose to continue working on this title if you're ready to put it up for sale.
- Tick the box next to "I confirm that I have legal rights..." and click "Put On Sale."
- Unlike Amazon's KDP, you do not get to choose your royalty option. For eBooks $2.99 to $9.99, it is a straight 65%, a little less than Amazon's 70% choice. For eBooks below and above these prices, it is a straight 40%, a little more than Amazon's 35% choice.

Marketing can be a full-time job alone, but for the working author, time spent marketing must be managed if you're to get any new content written. Take some time to learn your chosen social networks. Set a day aside every month to navigate, research, and update Duotrope, sending short stories out once again. Choose one day every week, like Sunday mornings, to write blog posts for the week and/or record podcasts.

Focus.

Write SOMETHING every day, and preferably, write four hours every day, with the exception of your Duotrope day, once a month.

Find a flow where you can intersperse your marketing in your writing. By utilizing automation and taking the time at the beginning to set all this up efficiently, you will be able to do the bulk of the marketing work in a few hours each week. The rest, tweet here and there. Check in at Starbucks. Upload a picture of something that inspired you.

Connect with people.

Plus.

Write. Write. Write. Market. Then write some more.

PART IV: AUTHOR ESSAYS

This section contains a collection of essays by authors who are both traditionally and self-published about their experiences in publishing and marketing their books.

ARE YOU RICH?
by Christine Rose

Often times at our events, I get asked this same question (usually by tweens) when they find out I'm an author.

They ask, "Are you rich?"

I have to really, really try not to laugh at that question. Really. Really. Try.

Sure, it's the kids who actually ask, but I don't doubt that many people assume that we are rich. Adults just know that it's not polite to ask someone about those things.

Still, this question is quite telling, it shows that a good portion of the public think that being an author = rich. Mansions. Movies. Chateau in France, etc.

Another one that gets me: "You should get them to make a movie of your book."

Hmmm. Great idea. Why didn't I think of that?

Or: "You should go on Oprah."

Yep. Got her on speed dial, how could that have slipped my mind?

Because when people think of authors, people think of *famous* authors like Stephen King, J. K. Rowling, Stephanie Meyer, James Patterson, etc.

Even I, just a short year ago, believed that if we could hit the much coveted New York Times Best Seller list, that we'd be doing okay.

Not.

Reality is most certainly a bitch.

For those of you who follow me on Facebook and/or Twitter, you know that Ethan and I now have a New York literary agent!

Yeah us!

Her name is Louise Fury with the L. Perkins Agency, and she's all kinds of awesome. I've started working on a YA Steampunk Romance that she'll be shopping around later this year.

Now that we have an agent, we have a better chance of being published by a NY Big Boy. That means, when she sells it, an advance and better distribution! Still, even with that coveted six-figure advance, we'll be far from "rich."

Just think: say we get a $100,000 advance, $85,000 of which we get to keep (15% to Louise), it's likely the only money we will ever see from that book because "an advance" means an advance against royalties. Big Boy Publishers offer between 5-7% in royalties. Let's take that large end at 7% on a moderately listed YA paperback novel of $8.99. That's $.63 a book, meaning the book would have to sell nearly 160,000 copies *just to break even* on the advance. The average books sells 500 copies. We've sold 5,000 copies over the last eighteen months in the Rowan series, which is about what a midlist author sells, even with a NY Big Boy.

If it takes me a year to write a book, that's 85k a year. Not bad, by any means, even for me and Ethan both.

That's the norm in publishing.

(And even that's changing. Read this post by twenty-year veteran author Robert J. Sawyer. He wrote "FlashForward." You might have seen the TV show, which is now canceled.)

But then let's take into account the five years it's taken us to get there without being paid any advances. That $85k/yr has just been averaged into $17K/yr for our first sale. Hopefully thereafter, I can be writing a book a year and making about $85/k every year for a single book. Still $100K is a huge advance. Most advances are more like $10-30k.

And that doesn't factor in that authors have to use *their own money* for publicity. The publisher doesn't help with that unless you are Stephanie Meyer or one of those other big names.

Seriously.

And this is all best case scenario with a NYBB. Being with an independent publisher, we get a higher % on book sales, but have a more limited distribution. We rarely make anything that we haven't hand-sold at an event. And over the past 18 months, we're consistently spending more than we're making on travel, fees, marketing, and just living.

I wouldn't be turning down even a $30,000 advance at this point.

If you're thinking about becoming an author so you can be rich? Think again.

You'll spend less money, have far less stress, and have just about the same odds by playing the lottery. In fact, I'm thinking more and more about that strategy.

So… No, little girl, I'm not rich. I'm surviving.

If you like our books, please support us by buying one instead of borrowing one.

(originally posted on our blog[1] August 4, 2010)

---

1 http://www.christineandethanrose.com/blog

I'M A WRITER
by Maxwell Cynn

"I'm a writer."

A lot of people say that. But I don't write to make a living, I live to write. It's like eating, sleeping, or sex. Being a writer is more akin to being a sculptor than an accountant. It's something that comes from within, unbidden, uncontrolled. Though it is possible to learn the technical aspects of writing, there must be a spark that transforms writing into literary art. But none of that really matters toward being published, and being published is the aspiration of most writers.

Publishing is a business. Publishing revolves around packaging, marketing, and selling books. That's a hard lesson for many writers to learn. Like many emerging authors I naively believed that the words are what sells books. Unfortunately, that is rarely the case. Some of the best writing sits unwanted in slush piles, or is published in short runs by small presses, while mediocre scribble hits the best seller lists.

Great writing is still great writing, but many great artists have died in obscurity, their genius only recognized later, and literature is in its essence a form of art. Yet, great writing stands the test of time, while many bestsellers are forgotten in a few months or years. As artists, writers seek the sublime heights of classic literature, but writers also need to make a living.

Writers, all artists really, live in two worlds; following the call of their muse, while seeking recognition for their hard work. The two are, unfortunately, mutually exclusive and they must be addressed separately. Though the art of literature is very personal and cannot be learned, writers must train the skills which allow them to transfer to the page what they hold inside. I cannot emphasize enough the importance of learning the technical aspects of the craft.

As a writer, I've taken many creative writing courses, and attended seminars on writing, but the best courses, the ones that improved my writing the most, were journalism courses. Journalism focuses on the tools of the trade, more than the art of writing. But all of the creative writing courses in the world cannot teach someone how to be a writer, and as I said before, the greatest writer remains unread unless they are published.

A writer must come to terms with the other side of writing, the business side. Many writers spend a great deal of time developing their art and very little developing their knowledge of publishing. Again, and I can't say it often enough, publishing is a business. Once a reader buys a book the writing becomes important. If they love the writing, they look for more, they tell their friends, they stand in line to meet the author, they become fans. If they don't like it, they can also be virulent detractors. But first they must buy the book.

Readers buy books for many reasons, most of which have little to do with the writing. They may have heard about the author from friends, liked the cover art, or were intrigued by the back-cover blurb or reviews, but they are buying the book without knowing whether or not it is well written. They buy because of marketing, that dark side of writing which literary artists don't care to think about. It is the business of publishing to sell books, not to provide literary art.

Granted, it is important that, once a reader buys a book, they like it. The good reviews and word of mouth sell more books. That's good marketing, but we need to separate marketing from art. A good salesman can sell a bad product, but a poor salesman couldn't sell Shakespeare. At the level of sales, quality only effects future sales, and business is focused on now. The product must reach the consumer before the after-effects of good writing can be realized.

A writer must stay true to their art and make it the best it can be, but they must also become market savvy if they ever want to see their work in print. Great literature, after all, does not sell itself. Even on the level of pitching to agents and publishers, most projects are undertaken without a full reading of the work. The editing process can do wonders, even with a mediocre manuscript, if the concept and author are marketable.

Even after an agent has agreed to represent a writer, and a publisher has bought the rights to publish one or more of the writer's manuscripts, the dichotomy continues. A writer is at once working with an editor to produce a work of literary art, and with a marketing team to sell themselves and their work. And that duet of responsibility doesn't end once the copy goes off to the press. There remains promotion of the book, and of course, writing the next manuscript.

As a writer, it is disheartening to realize more and more of my time is spent marketing, leaving less time for writing. Yet as a writer, selling my work is the work at hand. It is the business of writing that pays the bills, but more importantly to the artist, it is the business of writing which allows literary works to reach an audience.

With the realization of the business aspects of being a professional writer come many options and decisions, and making informed decisions requires knowledge of the publishing business. As I said before, readers buy books for diverse reasons; agents and editors do as well. A writer's greatest asset, and one they can build and nurture, is a fan base. But how does a writer build that base before their book is published?

A writer's primary tool is words and there are many levels to being published along with many outlets for a writer's work. The novel is perhaps the most difficult to sell, and expensive to produce, form of literature. When a publisher buys rights to a novel, it is a huge investment with an uncertain return. But when an editor acquires a piece for a magazine it is less of an expense, and the magazine itself has a certain readership, so the editor is willing to take more risk. That simple fact of business means it is easier for an unknown writer to publish in magazines.

Today there are limitless outlets for short stories and articles, from blogs and eZines to major print magazines and anthologies. Many such outlets offer no pay, or token payment, but a writer's name and work is made available to the reading public, which builds a fan base. Others pay quite well, for more established writers. But it is the writer's name and reputation on the byline, whether it is a short blog post or a high paying feature article, so it must be a work of literary art. That reputation brings me to the subject of self-publishing.

Vanity presses, those who publish at the author's expense, have always been looked down on in the publishing industry and many consider self-publishing to be equivalent to vanity publishing. But self-publishing can get a writer's name out to readers, and writers can even make good money at it. Yet, as I've pointed out, it is the writer's name and reputation on the byline. A self-published work must be as good, or better, than what the big houses in New York produce. And even then, some print publishers will look askance at a self-published author.

Another concern with a writer self-publishing is they must take on the responsibility of being the publisher. That responsibility includes professionally editing, designing, and marketing a book. Some writers do quite well wearing both hats, as writer and publisher, but it is often difficult enough for artists to think like businesspeople and a publisher must be completely comfortable with the business side of publishing. But the modern ease of self-publishing, in my opinion, is the greatest development for writers since the printing press, and it is bringing about a paradigm shift in the art of writing, and how literary art reaches the public.

*****

Maxwell Cynn is the author of two eBooks, *ArchAngelxx* and *CybrGrrl*, available on Amazon Kindle. He has also published a number of short stories and essays, both online and in print, including stories in recent issues of *The Absent Willow Review* and *Fissure Magazine*. He currently writes for several literary blogs and continues to write novels and short fiction. Max, his books, and all his social networks, can be reached through links on his website, MaxwellCynn.com.

Books: *ArchAngelxx, CybrGrrl*
Website & Blog: http://www.MaxwellCynn.com
Twitter: @MaxwellCynn
Facebook (FB): /maxwellcynn[1]

---

1 Facebook will be abbreviated FB when necessary. The "/maxwellcynn" and similar tags for other authors denotes that this comes after the main website; e.g., http://www.facebook.com/maxwellcynn.

RIDING THE TORNADO
By Helen Ginger

Writers today feel like they've followed the yellow brick road only to find themselves trapped under the house with the wicked witch in a land where agents reject new writers without reading their submissions, publishers only consider established writers or celebrities, and editors expect work to be publication-ready. What they've actually done is whip back the curtain and seen reality: most submissions do get rejected based on the query, publishers prefer a sure deal, and your work has to be as near to perfection as you can get it. Reality is scary.

Some decide to set out alone on the yellow brick road. They turn to self-publishing. Nothing wrong with that. In fact, more and more writers are doing it. They still have to produce a book with compelling characters, a fascinating plot, and twists and turns that keep the reader guessing. Anything less and readers won't buy the next book and, via the internet, will encourage others not to buy the first one.

Whether you're going to walk the brick road by yourself, hook up with a small or regional publisher, or gather an agent/editor/marketing team, more of the work than ever before falls on your shoulders.

1. Once you've written, torn apart, and rewritten your book, you need to get a freelance editor to go through it. Then once you've gotten it back and picked yourself up off the floor, you have to work with that editor to get the manuscript ready to submit.

2. While you're writing and rewriting, you have to establish your platform. You cannot wait until the book is out. If no one knows you, few will buy the book. Blog, tweet, friend others, participate in email groups, guest post and comment on other blogs, share on book review sites, link up on LinkedIn, make virtual friends. While you're at it, make in-person friends, like the CRM in your local bookstore or members of the local chapter of Sisters In Crime or Story Circle Network or whatever group fits with the genre you're writing. Build up your credits by getting published in another genre or in an anthology, a newspaper,

a magazine. Enter (and hopefully win) a writing contest. Go to conferences and meet other writers, agents and editors - give out business cards, keep in touch.

3. Don't rush the query letter. Too many agents and editors stop reading halfway through the query. They reject before they get to the sample pages. Write and re-write, then when it's perfect, get your editor to read it. Then once you've picked yourself up off the floor...get back to work.

When you decide to become a writer, you have to do more than write. You have to edit, promote, network, speak, read, smile until your lips hurt, learn how to do things you've never heard of, let alone want to know, and perhaps most important, be ready to step off that yellow brick road. It can get crowded with all the people wanting to be an author. Be ready to leave the worn path and map your own road to success.

Whatever you decide, becoming a published author is rarely easy. It is, however, worth the work when you hold your book and run your fingertip along the title.

*****

Helen Ginger is the author of three nonfiction books with TSTC Publishing in their TechCareers series and is writing a women's fiction book. She's a freelance editor and writing coach for other fiction authors and a Marketing Director for Legends In Our Own Minds®. When she started writing this article, Helen sent out a tweet to her followers and asked what they would like to hear from an editor. Her favorite response came from @Robert_Dean: "I didn't hate it."

Books: *Computer Gaming, Avionics, Automotive Technicians*
Website & Editing Services: http://helenginger.com
Blog: http://straightfromhel.blogspot.com
Twitter: @MermaidHel * **LinkedIn**: /helenginger * **FB**: /HelenGinger1
Goodreads: http://www.goodreads.com/user/show/1015487
Legends In Our Own Minds®: http://legendsinourownminds.com

ADVICE FROM MY PUBLISHED
TO MY UNPUBLISHED SELF
by Skyler White

Me Now: Hi.

Me That Was: Oh my god! How'd you get here? What are you doing? And what in the name of all that's holy happened to your hair?

Me Now: Shut up. It's a busy week. And I only have an hour, so if you want to ask me anything about what's coming now that you've sold your first book, you'd better get going.

MTW: Oh. OK. I just did my annual "Year Ahead" tarot reading, and it says I'm a fool. A rank beginner! It suggests that very few of the skills I developed as an aspiring writer translate into life as a published writer, and that the whole industry is a mysterious new world whose most basic rules and physics I don't know.

MN: There's a lot of truth to that. This is why you'll be very glad you have an agent. She's invaluable for answering questions about protocol, about when to ask your editor something, vs when to ask your publicist, vs when to just keep it to yourself.

MTW: I have a publicist!

MN: Congratulations. And she has you. And several hundred other writers.

MTW: Oh.

MN: On the other hand, everything you've learned about writing still counts, but don't stop working on it. Make sure you keep getting better as a writer. When you get reviewers who don't like your work, it'll comfort you to know you're not done improving.

MTW: Oh my god! Reviewers! I hadn't even thought about that. What's that like?

MN: It feels a lot like getting judges' feedback from contests. One judge will hate, one will love. The big differences are that the score sheets are public, there are more of them, and they turn up in your Google alerts with no warning or pattern.

MTW: I'll probably end up checking every five minutes compulsively.

MN: It would really be better if you didn't. (But you will.)

MTW: But the bad ones won't bother me as much right?

MN: (fiddles with shoelaces)

MTW: Oh. Ok. Maybe by the third book?

MN: Maybe.

MTW: Oh wait! Oh my god, you've seen the cover! Will I like it? What does it look like? How does all that work?

MN: You'll get lucky. But you'll make friends with some folks who didn't, and it matters. What your cover looks like is important. Luckily, you have an editor who really gets what you're trying to do, and is able to explain what's needed at the cover conference.

MTW: There's a cover conference? Can I go?

MN: No. And don't ask to be invited. (But you will.)

MTW: Aww... but my cover feels like the most important thing about my book-to-be. It will be my writing's first impression on reviewers and reader, and I have no control over it!

MN: Yes, that's right. No control. The days of complete control over your book were over the minute you sold it.

MTW: But ...

MN: But it's better with help. Your editor improves both books, and the copywriter does the same. And a cover is primarily marketing tool. You have to let the people who know marketing do it. They write the back cover copy too.

MTW: No! But I'm the writer.

MN: Yeah, and you do get input. But you're going to get really lucky with the cover for "Falling," so you can stop making yourself crazy about that. You'll spend a lot of time you don't have creating a power point presentation of words and images for your editor to take into the cover conference, but you really don't need to. She gets the book and will be able to explain what the cover needs. After that the visual people do the visual work. And they nail it. Really. They give Olivia stone wings. They also give her a knife, which you'll never quite figure out since there's not one in the book, but you won't care because you'll love the wings and the design on her corset. But do the whole power point thing again for the second book anyway.

MTW: Cool. What do I need to know about promotion?

MN: There's a direct link between how much they pay for your book and how much they spend. They got you pretty cheap. They're not going to spend much. Your publicist isn't going to take hours crafting a customized marketing plan to get the word out about this brand new writer. She will send out galleys to long-lead reviewers, and books to a list she already has. But, she will also send copies to reviewers who aren't on her standard mailing if you give her a qualified list with mailing addresses. Spend some serious time crawling the web for book bloggers who review vampire fiction. One or two of these will become advocates for you. There is nothing more valuable than these people.

MTW: Ok, what else should I know?

MN: Blurb time will sneak up on you. Your editor will have some ideas and some in-house contacts, but now would be a great time to start cultivating friendships among published authors and asking if they'd be willing to blurb you. Don't be afraid to take that up yourself, your editor is busy.

MTW: OK. I've read that you should spend at least half your first advance, if not the whole thing, on promotion. So I was thinking about book trailers and bookmarks, or maybe temporary tattoos, and post-cards, and give-aways, and a website....

MN: OK, play this game with me. Pick one of the above.

MTW: Temporary tattoos.

MN: What benefit do you expect to get from them?

MTW: They'll be a cool promotion, a little unusual, and get people interested in the book.

MN: And what if they don't? What if I can tell you they'll end up having no promotional value you can trace? Would you do them anyway? Would they be fun, or useful, or educational in their own right beyond whatever promotional value they may or may not have?

MTW: Well, I'd make temporary versions of Olivia's tattoo. Considering what it says, I think people's reactions to them might make a good story.

MN: Then do it. (It turns out you're right.) But anything you do, do it because there's some benefit you know you're going to get, but the promotional value is always a gamble. Your best friend and your husband will conspire to build you a surprise book trailer. You'll have a launch party, and you'll build the tattoo gallery, and you'll never know if either sold a single book. But the tattoos will be really illuminating, and the party will make up for forty years of birthdays that fall three days before Christmas. So it's not really money wasted.

MTW: What about cons? I want to start going to cons!

MN: Cons get expensive fast. Now, after a year of doing it, my rule for myself is not to go to cons I'm not invited to. Even though I enjoyed them, and even though I made some wonderful friends. I'm not sorry I went last year. As a promotion tool though, I think they're a bust. Go because they're fun and you love connies.

MTW: Shouldn't I start a blogging, or tweeting or something?

MN: Same rule applies. If you get non-promotional value from blogging and tweeting, go for it. If you don't, don't. But remember resources are limited. You only have so much time and money. Writing toward a deadline is a big change. And there's more non-next-book-writing work than you expect , so you're going to have to get good at protecting your time. Way later than you'd like, you'll get some very good advice from Holly Black. She'll tell you "you know what sells your back list? Your front list. Write the next book."

MTW: Why does it all sound like you're still figuring this out??

MN: Because I am. You have this idea that once you cross the Published line, that you'll know stuff just by virtue of having sold, but it's not the case. When you started out as a writer, you spent a lot of time figuring out how you write best, investigating your own process. Try to have the same kind of patience and curiosity about how you publicize your writing.

MTW: Blah. I want answers. Make it easy for me.

MN: OK. Here are ten things you should know:

There are things only other writers understand or want to hear about in the length and detail you want to discuss them. Maintain and add to your writer friendships.

Don't waste your time watching your numbers or your sales rank. You will. Obsessively. But try not to. It's not who you want to be.

Protect your focus. Fiercely.

Some writers are plotters, some are pantsers. Do what you love. Know who you are. And do it because you love it and because it's who you are. Be as authentic in your publicity as you are in your writing.

No publicity you do matters, or if it does, it matter in some un-trackable, aggregate way, so do what you love. (Hint: It's probably writing.)

There is no Right Way. Stop looking. Experiment.

Write the next book.

In the Amazon present and the E-book future, book bloggers are new best signal-from-noise filter. They're the modern analog to the children's librarian thirty years ago who knew what you'd read, what you'd loved, and what you needed next.

Seeing your books on the shelf is every bit as cool as you think it will be. Getting letters from readers is even cooler.

MTW: Shouldn't there be ten things? Nine is such a weird number.

MN: Yeah, but you're running out of time.

MTW: Er, can I get some help?

MN: Sure.

MTW: OK out there, any of you have questions I should ask my future self? Bueller? Anyone at all?

*****

Skyler White crafts challenging fiction for a changing world. Her dark writings, populated with angels and devils, rock stars, scientists and revolutionaries, explore the secret places where myth and modernity collide.

Books: *and Falling, Fly; In Dreams Begin*
Website: http://skylerwhite.com
FB: /SkylerWhiteAuthor

SOCIAL NETWORKING FOR NON-FICTION AUTHORS[1]
By Charles Herbert Brown

Authors can no longer afford to be just authors. In order to succeed today, they must also become marketers.

Publishing contracts are harder to get than ever. The risks are simply too high for most houses to take a risk on an unknown (or even well-known) author, without a solid means to market the book once it comes off the printing press.

Even well-established authors, who want to attempt a new project on a topic they have never written on before, find that their track record does not easily translate into a publishing contract in another field.

The name of the game is all about establishing a "platform" as a way to sell your book.

What is a platform? Your platform is your marketing vehicle that leverages whatever recognition you have already established into book sales. A platform can be your network, your mailing list, or your fame or your followers on Twitter.

If you happen to host a popular TV or radio show, your show is your platform. If you are famous as an expert within your specialized niche, your mini-celebrity status is your platform. If you just left public office in disgrace, your infamy can be your platform (sorry).

If you successfully landed an airplane on the Hudson, or rescued yourself from a boulder that had pinned your arm for 127 hours (like Chesley Sullenberger or Aron Ralston), your newsworthiness is your platform.

Simply put, authors with platforms get published, and sell books.

Social networking is possibly the best, fastest and least expensive way for today's authors to build a platform (with the possible exception of the previously-mentioned leaving public office under a cloud of scandal).

---

1 The information herein also applies to fiction authors.

With that said, let's look at a five step process to building a durable platform for non-fiction writers:

Start a blog on the same topic of your book. What is a blog? A blog is a website that is designed to be easily updated with new content, even if you lack any technological skills. Most blogs are built on templates like Word press or Blogger, which make them extremely easy to create and use.

What if you already have a blog devoted to your life and family misadventures? Great, that blog can work in tandem with your new, specialized blog, but you still need to create a blog specifically devoted to your book.

Use your blog to make the writing process easier. Write one small post at a time. Don't worry about the order in which each topic will appear in your book, just write 500 to 1500 word posts as soon as you are ready to write about that subject.

You are actually writing your book on your blog and inviting the world to read it and give you feedback as a work in progress.

Invite reader comments. Ask readers for help when you get stuck with areas of research. Ask them for their own experiences and stories to be included in your finished product. Make them feel a part of your writing process.

Listen to their feedback and ideas. Some you will want to include in your book. Other comments will alert you to areas that need deeper explanation.

Engage your readers and respond to their input. Let them feel they are participating in the writing of your book and you can be sure they will gladly buy it when it comes out.

Your blog cannot attract readers in a vacuum. Get the word out about your blog with other social networking tools like Facebook, Twitter and LinkedIn. Whenever you write a new blog post, send out a Tweet or write an update on Facebook or LinkedIn.

Be sure to set up a separate Facebook "page" devoted to your topic. Don't try to roll your informal Facebook profile that use to connect with friends and family. There may be some overlap, but make sure you have two distinct presences on Facebook.

Engage and make friends. Not only might these people provide ideas and anecdotes you could incorporate in your book (with their permission of course) but they may also tell others about it and do much of the marketing for you.

You want to use social media to build your network and list of prospective book buyers. You also want to build anticipation for your book before it is ever published.

The more engage in social networking, the more readers, and subscribers, you will attract to your blog.

As you get familiar with Twitter, Facebook and LinkedIn, you will notice that people using these platforms have a tendency to form groups around common interests. Bloggers also form alliances based on their subject areas.

Join groups related to your books subject and ask questions for your research. On Twitter, follow other people who are interested in your topic. Start conversations with these people, get to know them, respond to their tweets and updates as well.

You will be amazed at how many of the big name experts in your field are blogging and tweeting. In the offline world, it is very difficult to get on these people's radar. But if you occasionally tweet about an article said expert wrote and include links to these articles, you will get noticed.

You may even form friendly enough relationships to land an interview with the expert who never would have responded to your request in the offline world.

Don't look on other bloggers as competitors, look at them as colleagues. If someone else has an excellent blog, write comments on their blog. Better yet, mention their blog on your own, encourage your readers to also read that person's blog.

Generosity is a valuable asset in the social networking community.

At some point, after your book is completed, you will want reviewers to write about your book. But it is hard to get reviewed in the New York Times, or any other offline publication, when you are a relatively unknown.

But these offline reviewers keep tabs on who is being talked about among the blogging community. If several bloggers with whom you have formed friendly relationships blog reviews about your book, it will be a lot easier to be found by the more prestigious offline world.

Build these friendships with random acts of support and feedback.

At some point you will want to approach a publisher (unless you are planning to self publish). If you have done all the things we've talked about so far, your query can include a reference to your blog, mentioning the number of readers you have. You can also mention the number of people who have "liked" your Facebook Page, and the number of Twitter followers you have.

If you can demonstrate that you have an audience for your book, even before it comes out, you will have a massive advantage over other prospective authors.

Keep blogging and tweeting. When your book is published, this is not time to stop. Keep writing blog posts about the book and your subject area (you may want to write another book on the same topic, so you don't want to lose these followers).

Blog about where you will be for book signings, blog about favorable reviews you receive, and enlist your readers to help you book more signings and get more reviews.

Make sure your social networking activities are not all about you, your blog, and your book. Promote others and their activities as well. Be a friend. If you find other people with good blogs, tell your followers to follow these people as well.

Networking, whether online or off, is about making friends and uplifting others. Believe me; generosity is rewarded on Twitter, Facebook and LinkedIn.

If you continue your blogging long after the book is written, it will keep your platform (and network) alive and well for your next book, not to mention possible speaking engagements. Your blog and book will position you as an expert in your field and open many more doors for you in the future.

Don't let social networking confuse you. Twitter, Facebook, LinkedIn and blogs are built to be easy to learn and use. If you get stuck at any point along the way, search Google and YouTube for tutorials on Word press, Twitter, LinkedIn or whatever you wish to learn more about.

But above all, use these platforms as a means to make friends and expand your network of people who share your interest in your chosen field or topic.

*****

Charles Brown helps people learn how to promote their brand, business, organization or cause with social media.

Website: http://webmarketingcoach.blogspot.com/
Twitter: @charbrown
FB: /SMMCafe
LinkedIn: /webmarketingcoach
BlogTalkRadio: /smmcafe

THE MTV/AMERICAN IDOL EFFECT IN WRITING
By Rhonda Eudaly

Once upon a time it was enough for authors to write a brilliant story, have it published, and be exalted all without leaving their homes. It was, once, "sexy" for an author to be a hermit or to sit in cafes in exotic places and commune with other artistic types. Those days are over.

MTV and American Idol (depending on your generation) changed everything. It was no longer enough to be talented. The musician now had to be "beautiful" and buff. Music videos meant singing, dancing, and entertaining on levels not previously seen before. American Idol reinforces the idea of having the "whole package" as a performer, and not just killer chops—a musician now has to put on a show instead of simply singing/playing.

This is the same for writers—and more. Many new writers think they can emulate the "classic" authors, write in a cave, and all will be well. This is no longer true. Smaller author lists, dwindling marketing budgets, and fewer marketplaces now require authors to be "Whole Package Writers." We must do so much more than write brilliantly. The project is just the beginning—regardless of size - or type - of publisher.

Writers—both new and established—are required to be marketers, promoters, editors, and entertainers. More and more books are sold online or in person. Publishers now look for writers who can create their own demand for their books by an active and entertaining online and in person presence, by being on the convention circuits, and doing whatever it takes to create more demand for the books.

I have a lot of short stories with small presses—I sell 85% of all my books in person at conventions. This means I have to be a performer. The other 15% is online or OTHER AUTHORS selling the books at conventions. I have to be charming, personable, and ready to talk to complete strangers at a drop of a hat. I also have to sometimes do things—like improv—to help make readings or panels more fun and exciting.

It's not always easy. I can get intent on what I'm doing and be a bit impatient and snappy—but I'm getting better (I hope). There's an expectation of approachability when I'm at a convention that I have to respect and accept and deal with gracefully. The same applies to online behavior.

Facebook and Twitter have made it so much easier to reach a lot of people quickly and inexpensively. A smart writer has a presence on all the social networks, as well as having a website/blog. A wise writer knows how to not tick people off by over-promoting your books or engaging in offensive online behavior. It's okay to mention your books, stories and interviews—in fact it would be foolish not to mention them, and include links—just NOT multiple times a day without anything else to buffer it. Readers want to know more about the author than just pitches to buy something—but they also don't need to know what you're eating for every meal. Just keep a nice balance between posts. It's really all about common sense. Think in terms of what bugs you about social networking, and don't do that.

Social networking has boomed as a marketing tool because it's free. Most writers—and let's face it, a lot of publishers—don't have the skills, time, or budget for a large scale marketing. It's important to come up with cost-conscious ways to market our work. Online is pretty much the most budget-savvy way, but there are ways to put out the "gimme" stuff—bookmarks, pens, postcards, etc—without having to eat ramen to pay for it. For the severely budget-constrained, you can make a lot of your own marketing materials with a decent color printer.

Bookmarks, postcards, and business cards are easy to do on your own. There are some ways to get those in perforated forms so the heavy lifting of cutting is done for you. In the past, I made pens with clear return address labels and packing tape. We built notebooks from small spiral bound memo books and stickers.

They're not sexy, but they get the job done. Then as your budget increases, so does the quality—shop around and you can get really good deals. I had pens screen printed for 80% off—which netted me good, professional looking ink pens for under $100. It takes time to do the research and the comparison shopping, but the payoff is worth the effort.

It's not easy, but it is necessary. This is something now required of all writers across the board. We are the whole package now. If we don't do it, no one else will. Besides, who has more to gain from the effort of your book than you?

*****

Rhonda Eudaly lives in Arlington, Texas where she's worked in offices, banking, radio, and education to support her writing. She's married with dogs and a rapidly growing rubber duck collection. She likes to spend time with friends and family, movies, and reading. Her two passions are writing and music.

Rhonda Eudaly has both fiction and non-fiction stories published in anthologies, magazines, and websites. Check out her website for her latest publications and downloads.

Books: *When The Party's Over, The Four Redheads: Apocalypse Now!*
Website & Blog: http://rhondaeudaly.com
Twitter: @reudaly
FB: reudaly
LinkedIn: /rhondaeudalysimpson

USING PUBLIC SPEAKING TO MARKET YOUR BOOK
by Denniger Bolton

Your willingness to do "whatever it takes" to reach your goals is the key ingredient to success in any endeavor. However, most writers I know, not all but most, are solitary souls spending their days in front of the laptop working on their craft. They have a narrow comfort zone, and are not willing to move beyond it, especially if they don't have to. Public speaking however, will yank all but a few out of their zones.

Are you willing to push beyond your zone, to do whatever it takes to give a speech to an audience of dozens, maybe hundreds? Getting up in front of people is the greatest fear there is, coming in ahead of dying even. Scary, but profitable.

Contemplate this: if you could overcome this almost innate fear, and you could make lots of money having as much fun possible with your clothes on, wouldn't you at least consider it?

In my book/seminar, "How to Write, Publish & Make a Living from Your Book – In 7 Easy Steps," (due out in Summer 2011), I go into detail about marketing, and stress the importance, especially for self-publishers, of direct marketing.

Wholesaling books for the most part means selling through bookstores, where everyone wants a cut. Distributors, wholesalers, the bookstore itself, all want a piece of the pie. The author is lucky to get a 10% slice. For the shy writer, allowing others to do the selling, he or she has taken the path of least resistance, a path which does not allow for optimum profits. There is an alternate route to making a much greater return on your investment, and that is to sell directly to the end user, which in the case of your book, is to your reader.

There are three methods, a three-legged stool that authors can utilize to sell directly to the reader.

Leg # 1 – One-on-One, or face to face selling, involving setting up a booth or table at a market, trade show, festival (including book festivals), or any place where you meet face to face with the person buying your book. I've set up on sidewalks and sold my books at coffee shops.

Leg #2 – Sales made from your website. Unlike Amazon or Barnes & Noble's websites, who take a 55% cut, when you sell from your own site, you eliminate all middlemen, collecting all the profits.

Leg #3 – The sales made through public speaking engagements.

Let's take a look at one leg of direct selling, public speaking, and how it might help you to sell more books for the highest possible return on investment. For more in depth coverage on all three methods, including selling your books through speaking engagements, as well as one-on-one sales and sales from your website, please check out the "projects" page of my website, www.dennigerbolton.com, where I will keep updated information on the release of the book mentioned earlier.

You are needed. Organizations such as Rotary and Kiwanis, book clubs and any organization that offers weekly or monthly programs, hire speakers to fill those time frames. There are writers I know who use the free speech/back of the room sales method and do really well, selling dozens and even hundreds of books at their talks. A big advantage over book signings at a bookstore is the profit are yours to keep, and many times there's a free meal, albeit of the rubber chicken variety.

Public speakers give their talks, or presentations, for free with the understanding that they will be allowed to offer their books for sale at the back of the room.

What do you need? Well, you've written a book, yes? You're an expert. You're an artist. You've written what you know. In your speech, you merely shifting delivery forms and instead of the written word, you tell out loud what you know.

First step, you need to write a speech. Plenty of books tell you how to do just that. Plenty books on presentation skills as well. Fortunately, the more talks you give, the better you'll get at it. Toastmasters is a great place to learn to comfortably give a speech. Go to http://www.toastmasters.org to find a club near you.

Attend some meetings of the Rotary or other associations as a guest, and listen to the presenters.

Develop a one-sheet, which like the name implies, is a single sheet of paper that you give to the meeting planner or the program director so they know a little bit about you and what your speech will be about.

So, what do you speak about? If you've written a non-fiction book, there is always the subject of your book. For fiction, you can talk about the writing process or how you came to write this book. I write mysteries, so I could talk about mysteries. I actually have a talk that I give to book clubs called, "Flatfeet, Snoops & Private Eyes." I do readings and give background on the top 10 Greatest Mysteries of All time.

Since I have this upcoming book on publishing, I have a speech called, "The Paradigm Shift in Publishing," which gives facts about the state of our changing industry, the rise of print on demand, eBooks, Kindle, self-publishing vs. traditional vs. vanity presses vs. publishing co-ops.

There is the writing process, marketing, or anything related to your book. Book readings are fine as well, but make entertaining.

Booking talks. Any organization that offers programs has a need for speakers. Some fill 15 minute slots, while others offer an hour. Good to know how much time they require of you before you start talking. Your talk fills a need. You are doing them a favor. Most of the time public speakers don't get paid, but some do. Some organizations offer an honorarium of $50 to a few hundred dollars. It's just a bonus if you do get paid as far as I'm concerned.

Back of the Room (BOR). Be sure to mention during your talk that you'll be "signing" books at the table after the program, and you can handle cash, checks, credit and debit cards. "After this talk I'll be at the back, (just make sure the audience has to pass by your table on the way out), so stop by if you want to talk or have me autograph your book."

If you haven't gotten your book out yet, you can take orders. Collect the money if you are within a month of the shipping date, and have a way to contact the buyer to keep them updated.

Prizes of books are good. Everybody wants to win something. You can do a drawing and collect business cards with email addresses to build up your database.

Writing your speech. We've all heard boring speeches, so come up with one that is not, boring that is. Humor is good. A few jokes are good. I like topical humor, which comes out of the meeting of which your speech is a part. Listen to the announcements, the trials and tribulations the group is going through. Be open to insert your humorous comment. Toastmasters is a great and fun place to learn this talent. Like writing, the more talks you give, the better you will get at it. I guarantee that even if you are uncomfortable to start, you will find that after a while you really dig speaking, and will want to do more of it.

Delivering your speech. I'm of the opinion that the best speech is the most natural. Relax. Be yourself. Emphasize some words so you don't sound stale, monotone and thus boring. Make eye contact. Find some folks here and there around the room and talk to them, but don't stay with one person too long. And don't lose focus. And don't forget to breathe.

Going pro. Speaking and writing books go hand in hand. Your book becomes a calling card to booking paid speeches, and your speech a venue to selling books.

As a professional, you can make a few hundred to several thousand dollars delivering a speech. Check out a Tony Robbins seminar to get an idea of how much money there is in this business. One rule of thumb is that the more customized the speech is to the group, the more money you can expect to make. Like anything else, you will make more as time goes by.

When can you expect to make money from your free speeches? Simple. When someone says, "How much do you charge?"

Seminars & workshops. You can use your free speech to not only sell your books but to sell or collect leads for your seminar/workshop. And when you put on your seminar, you can sell your books BOR. How synchronistic is that?

Consider adding speeches to your marketing mix. It's profitable and it's fun.

*****

Ever since he was 14 years old, **Denniger Bolton** knew he would grow up to be a writer. Like everything else in his life, it just took him some time to realize it. More decades than he'd care to admit.

Denniger has written three mystery/adventure novels, runs his own publishing house, and gives workshops on self-publishing.

Books: *Hippie Hollow: Murder on a Nude Beach; The Armadillo Whisperer: Murder Behind Bars; Honk if You're Jesus: Murder by the Bay*
Website & Blog: http://dennigerbolton.com
Publishing Co: http://javelinabooks.com
Email: denniger@javelinabooks.com
Twitter: @javelinabooks
FB: /dennigerbolton

PUBLISHING REALITIES: A STIKMANZ TALE
by Robert Stikmanz

Young student athletes are often spooned a dose of reality therapy known as the "One Percent Rule." The reality of sports, the youth are told, is that only one percent of high school varsity athletes will be offered a college athletics scholarship, and of that select few, only one percent will play even a single professional season. Whether or not there is a genuinely scientific basis for this claim, the sense of it holds water and the message is clear: play because you love the sport, not because you think talent and hard work lead inevitably to riches. Likely, they will not.

A similar check on illusions, youthful or otherwise, can be made for the world of big corporate publishing, although one percent is probably an inflated estimate of the number of aspiring authors who will ever sign a contract with a major house. The mere fact of a winnowing process, however, is not necessarily bad. If the process always guaranteed publication of books of social or artistic merit it would be all to the good. Some works of this kind do pass through the sieve into print. Unfortunately, as review of a list of new titles from major houses reveals, the vast majority of books making it through the mill are familiar, formulaic and preformed for existing market categories. Obtaining a contract with a major house, or even getting professional representation, is unquestionably an accomplishment. Only rarely, though, is it an accomplishment based on originality or literary worth.

I am not one of the elect with a major publisher contract. That this is so was not for lack of trying. Over a period of several years, I shopped my first novel to agents and publishers with the discipline and persistence popular wisdom dictates. There were many, many heartening moments, but ultimately this was such an exercise in frustration that I abandoned the effort.

Over the course to date of my life as author of off-beat speculative fiction, I have consistently ignored every lick of practical advice available to aspiring writers. For instance, I have never bothered to research genres or sub-genres that might be experiencing popularity, much less written within their conventions. I have never analyzed a bestselling title with an eye to emulating its style, message or motifs. Never even once have I, before beginning to write, surveyed the publishing field to see if some editor in the back corner of a big corporate house might have shown a glimmer of interest in works remotely similar to the fiction that I produce. I have always written exactly what I have wanted to write, in the face of all consequences. Staying true to my vision as an artist has always taken precedence over making compromises in pursuit of a buck.

My largest failing from the perspective of the corporate publishing world appears to be that the fiction I choose to write does not fit a ready-made marketing category. In an industry in which genres are subject to ever finer slicing by marketing minds, a label like science fiction has fragmented into a sunburst of ever more specific sub-genres: cyberpunk, alternate history, steampunk, "hard" sci-fi, space fantasy, etc. The same kind of fracturing has taken place under the umbrella of fantasy, with adjectives like high, urban, future, and contemporary coming into play for the first level sort. Operating alongside a publishing milieu that happily brands a book "Paranormal Alternate History Space Fantasy," and then rejoices because flacks know how to pimp it, I have nevertheless forged forward across borders, grabbing elements from all the branches of fantasy and sci-fi to stir into a pot with large dollops from outside the field, such as magical realism, folk tales, beat poetry, absurdism, romance and westerns.

During the period in which I slowly checked off, one after another, every agent in the Association of Authors Representatives who signaled interest in speculative fiction, I received a high percentage of personal responses. At first I was encouraged by this. The evidence was clear that I framed queries and provided samples that were read. I accumulated a stack of responses that were variations on, "Dear Robert, this is good. Even very good. You are going to have no problem finding an agent to represent this work. Unfortunately, it is not the kind of material that I represent." A couple of times these rejections even included a referral. "This is not what I represent, but send it to X." The referrals sent personal responses, too. They also thought my work very good. Alas, it was not what they represented either. There came a time when I found the personal rejections more discouraging than form letters. That was the point at which I abandoned the search for an agent.

My next initiative was to troll the successively less prestigious levels of the publishing world willing to read un-agented queries. Many of these responses were also personal, and all of these were encouraging. No one ever questioned the quality of my fiction. Quite the contrary, I was told repeatedly that I have what it takes; however, my writing was never quite the kind that any of these houses publish.

A day came when I had to admit that I had pretty well exhausted possibility within the standard model. No matter that quite actually scores of industry professionals had told me my work is of high caliber, it became plain that I was not going to find an agent, and I was not going to sell my first novel representing myself.

Rather than admit defeat, consign my manuscript to the trash heap and look for a job selling insurance, I decided to self-publish. In 2000, I brought out the first edition of my first novel, *Prelude to a Change of Mind*, using a print-on-demand service. Surprisingly, given the barriers to promoting and distributing self-published titles, the book enjoyed enough success to keep my dreams alive. After six years of modest but steady sales, *Prelude to a Change of Mind* had obtained enough presence to attract attention from shadows on the fringes of the publishing industry.

There is a sad tale I could rehearse, and some day I shall. For now, I note only that it took a while, but I finally recognized there are those who prey on the dreams of writers hungry for publication. Even smart people can be fooled by the unscrupulous. This was, as we say in the South, my "Come to Jesus" moment. Fortunately, as I wondered what to do next, Christine and Ethan Rose approached me about bringing my work under their imprint, Blue Moose Press. Our discussions led to reorganization of BMP into what it is today, effectively an authors' publishing cooperative. We are feeling our way forward with this new structure, which remains very much a matter of learning as we go. Slowly, the initiative begins to pay dividends. Revised editions of my first two novels are now available through Blue Moose; my third novel is in process of revision. I cannot yet say the future looks bright, but I can say it is not lost in darkness. The greatest beauty of the effort is that I have been able to continue ignoring popular wisdom. I still write exactly the books that I want to write. Making common cause with other authors of talent and dedication I have found a means to escape the constraints of genre with an end run around the standard model. On the horizon I think I may even see a day when I'll make a buck.

*****

Robert Stikmanz is the creative identity of an author and artist long resident in Austin, Texas. A native of the gulf coast city of La Porte, and a graduate of Austin College (Sherman, TX), he began publishing poems and occasional illustrations in the late seventies. Moving to Austin in 1979 he became an active presence in independent Texas letters, contributing poems, short essays, illustrations, design and production assistance to numerous small press publications, including the Sleepy Tree anthologies, Window Magazine, The Argonaut, Aileron, VíAtzlan, Lone Star Socialist, SA, Austin Duckweed and Vowel Movement. Three collections of his poems are out of print, probably for the best: The Green Book (Sleepy Tree Publishing, 1981), 6 (Aileron Press Miniature, 1983) and Restless Native (Ambrose & Lewis, 1988).

Books: *Prelude to a Change of Mind, Entranscing, Sleeper Awakes*
Website & Blog: http://robertstikmanz.com
Twitter: @robertstikmanz
FB: /robert.stikmanz

APPENDIX

CHECKLISTS

Please use the following checklists as a quick-reference guide to help you navigate your publishing path and marketing strategy. They are organized in sections, starting with the most important place to start no matter where you are in the writing process or how close you are to finishing your manuscript.

Whether you choose to pursue the New York traditional route, self-publish through your own company, or go with a subsidy press, you should begin building your platform now. Even if your book is not finished, start building these networks now. Blog now. Three times a week. You cannot start doing this too soon. You want your readers to know you before your book comes out.

Remember, *connect* with your readers, don't try to impress them. Just be yourself. Be professional. And be entertaining. Leave elitism and entitlement off your networking platform.

CONNECT.

BUILDING A PLATFORM

- ❏ Create a folder called "Marketing" on your desktop for quick and easy access.
- ❏ Create a Marketing Info. document and save it in your "Marketing" folder, organized by book title; ex: "Rowan_Marketing."
- ❏ Create a URL document in which you will paste important URLs and shortcuts (like to your books and author profile using your Amazon Associates links).
- ❏ Write your author bios. Save them to your "Marketing" folder.
- ❏ Write your book blurbs, even if your book isn't finished. Many authors write their book blurbs before they write the book. It's easier to write a blurb on a high concept rather than trying to shrink those 80,000 words down into 50. "Marketing" folder.
- ❏ Get your author photos taken. Save them to your "Marketing" folder.
- ❏ Choose your favorite author photo and brand it by using it on Facebook, Twitter, Goodreads, anywhere you need an avatar. Remember, it needs to look like you if you want to be recognized.
- ❏ Reserve a URL (if you choose) http://www.yourname.com
- ❏ Open a WordPress (or Blogspot, etc.) account with your name; e.g., yourname.wordpress.com. Format with a theme that is eye-friendly and that reflects you. Personalize it.
- ❏ Find the RSS subscription URL for your blog and paste it in your URL document.
- ❏ Start a Twitter account with your name (or change your existing account to show your author name. Put your author-brand picture up in your profile.
- ❏ Follow industry professionals, other authors, and journalists. Build your follower list with TweetAdder or organically through #FF requests. Interact. Participate.
- ❏ Create a Facebook fan page. Author-brand photo on profile and fan page.

❑ Create a Goodreads and/or LibraryThing (et al.) author page. Author-brand picture in profile(s).

❑ Set up your Amazon Accounts (Associates, Author Central, KDP, etc.). Author-brand photo in Author Central. (You may not be able to create an Author Central page until after your book is already available via Amazon.com.

❑ If your book is already on Amazon, get your affiliate link to it and save it in your URL document.

❑ Brainstorm blog topics. Don't stop until you reach 100. Choose the top 15 and start writing. When you have six written, schedule them and make your blog live. Start tweeting, etc.

❑ Start a list of recurring tweets to promote you and your books/ works. Include Amazon Associates links when linking to Amazon. Save in your "Marketing" folder.

❑ Get Author cards printed. Business cards, club fliers, or bookmarks will work. Get them professionally printed. Include your blog, picture, and social networks. Include your book cover and maybe a book blurb, if ready. Have some with you always. Remember, NextDayFlyers has reasonably priced, high quality printing for "club flyers," postcards, bookmarks, and business cards.

❑ Start getting to know your local book sellers and librarians.

❑ Write a short story a week, if you can. If you're not working on a novel. At least one a month if you are. Send it out using Duotrope.com. Keep it out until it's published. Start on the next one. Repeat.

❑ Create an inspiration poster. This can be pieced together in Photoshop, if you have the skills, or pasted together from magazine clippings. This is a visual representation of your goals, your dreams, your motivations. Put it up where you can see it everyday.

❑ Write an "I will feel successful when..." reminder. For example: "I will feel successful when my blog gets 30 views a day." or "I will feel successful when I reach 50,000 words." Post it where you see it daily. Take it in baby steps. This is a ***long, long, arduous*** process. Give yourself benchmarks. Once you reach one goal, reward yourself. Then make another.

❑ It's very important to *feel* successful along the way. Do you feel successful? If not, brainstorm what will help you feel successful. Perhaps challenge your definition of "success."

NEW YORK BIG BOY

If you've chosen the NYBB publishing path, here are the steps you need to take to get there. Remember, this path can take years. Be patient with yourself and with the system. Be very, very flexible. Keep writing.

❑ Complete & polish your manuscript. That means hiring a professional editor to go over it.

❑ Write your query letter. Then revise it. Set it aside.

❑ Start researching agents. Make a list of your top ten, then your next ten, etc. Follow them on Twitter. Interact with them. Don't mention you're an author or tell them about your book. Twitter is not the place to query.

❑ Sign up for QueryTracker. Pay the $25.

❑ Read five Query Shark posts every day. At least. Until you've read it all. Follow @queryshark on Twitter.

❑ Read Nathan Bransford's blog. Five posts a day, until you're through the entire thing.

❑ Revise your query letter again. Ask people in your network to read it and offer comments/suggestions. Revise it again. Put it aside.

❑ Research writer conferences in your area. Go to one. Go to another. Talk to other writers. Network with agents. Ask questions.

❑ Read industry magazines. Subscribe to Publishers Weekly.

❑ Read industry blogs. Spend at least an hour a day keeping up with the market.

❑ Never stop writing. At least one hour a day, preferably four hours.

❑ Revise your query letter again. Send it out to your first round of agents (if they allow simultaneous submissions). Wait.

❑ Depending on your responses, polish query and repeat.

INDEPENDENT PUBLISHER

❑ Complete & polish your manuscript. That means hiring a professional editor to go over it.

❑ Write your query letter. Then revise it. Set it aside.

❑ Research Independent Publishers. When you have a list of your top ten, start contacting some of their authors and ask what it's like to work with them. Do they pay royalties on time? Advances? Etc.

❑ Remember, don't sign your rights away for nothing. Get at least a token advance if you're going with an Indie.

❑ Revise your query letter again. Ask people in your network to read it and offer comments/suggestions. Revise it again. Put it aside.

❑ Read industry blogs. Spend at least an hour a day keeping up with the market.

❑ Never stop writing. At least one hour a day, preferably four hours.

❑ Revise your query letter again. Send it out to your first round of publishers (if they allow simultaneous submissions). Wait.

❑ Depending on your responses, polish query and repeat.

"SELF-PUBLISHING"

This is the longest list, as you're doing it all yourself.

❑ Complete and polish your manuscript. That means hire a professional editor to go over it.

❑ Read industry blogs. Spend at least an hour a day keeping up with the market.

❑ Never stop writing. At least one hour a day, preferably four hours.

❑ Choose a business name and set up your business entity, whether that is a Sole Prop., General Partnership, or LLC.

- ❏ Set up your publishing account with Lightning Source, CreateSpace, or whichever printer/service you decide on.
- ❏ Research your market (either at a bookstore or on Amazon) and look for pricing information and styles of book covers.
- ❏ Set up crowdsourcing via Kickstarter or IndieGoGo to raise funds for professional services.
- ❏ Work with a cover artist to design your book cover to fit in with the current market.
- ❏ Set up an account with the Library of Congress.
- ❏ Copyright your work with the U. S. Copyright office.
- ❏ Set up an account with Bowker. Purchase at least ten ISBNs. Assign an ISBN to your title for the paperback and eBook.
- ❏ Choose your trim size[1]. A good size is 8.5 x 5.5, just slightly smaller than trade paperback size (6x9, the size of this book) for fiction. If it has over 80K words, you could go 6x9 and still have a substantial book. Under 80K, I recommend 8.5 x 5.5 or even 8x5, which is my new favorite trim size.
- ❏ Learn how to use InDesign, QuarkXpress, or another layout program, or hire a layout designer to layout your book.
- ❏ Apply for LCCN from the Library of Congress. Put it on the title page of your book. Look at other books to see the preferred format.
- ❏ Download the INDD cover template from LSI. Layout the compete cover in InDesign using that template and the included barcode. Insert the cover text in InDesign rather than Photoshop. It will be cleaner.
- ❏ Set up your title in LSI or CreateSpace & order a proof.
- ❏ Approve the proof, and order your books.
- ❏ Send two books along with a marketing plan to Diane Simowski at Barnes & Noble if you want them to carry your book in their warehouse. Remember, they have to be returnable with a 55% discount. This may not be possible with CreateSpace, but, again, bookstores are not your market yet.

---

1 trim size = the measurements of your finished book

❏ Either upload a document with clear formatting to Amazon's KDP for the Kindle or hire someone to convert your MS to eBook. Set up the title there.

❏ Set up your eBook on Smashwords and PubIt.

❏ Get the Amazon Associates links for your books once they go live on Amazon, and use those on your blog, in your tweets, and anywhere you link to your book.

❏ Start activating your local networks.

❏ Write up a press release, and send it out to local papers, book stores, and libraries.

VANITY PRESS

There is absolutely no reason to go with a Vanity Press, period. Even if you just want to see your book in print, go with CreateSpace or at the very least LuLu.

Don't pay anyone to publish your book.

REVIEWS

Reviews requests need to be sent out at least a month, preferable two or three, before your book is released.

❏ Compose a cover letter-style email pitching a review request. Save it as a draft. You will use it (Copy/Paste) frequently.

❏ Research blogs/review sites. Look for submission policies, if any.

❏ Make a list of top ten, next ten, etc.

❏ Start at the top and query your list.

❏ As reviews come in, start a new page on your blog titled "Reviews," or something more creative, and post snippets there with links back to the original, full review.

❏ Create new recurring Tweets with special reviews. Remember to set your recurring Tweets to update randomly and not more frequently than every two hours. No SPAM.

❏ Negative review? Don't respond. Just ignore it. It will be forgotten by next week. If you respond, you give it life.

BLOG TOUR

- ❑ Compose a cover letter-style email pitching your blog tour. Save it as a draft. You will use it (Copy/Paste) frequently.
- ❑ Research blogs. Look for submission policies, if any.
- ❑ Make a list of top ten, next ten, etc.
- ❑ Schedule a block of time for your blog tour.
- ❑ Start at the top and query your list, requesting specific days (for blog tours).
- ❑ Write up four or five guest posts and have them ready. If they give you a topic, all the better. You can use your pre-written posts on your own blog.
- ❑ As confirmations come in, create a blog post filling in your schedule with links to the respective blogs. Keep in draft form until complete.
- ❑ Schedule blog tour schedule for the day before your blog tour begins.
- ❑ Each day during the blog tour, post on your blog telling your readers where you are that day and what you'll be discussing.
- ❑ If you decided to make a book trailer on YouTube, during the blog tour is a great time to release it to the public.
- ❑ During your blog tour, Tweet often. Tweet creatively. Link back to your blog and to the guest blog, alternately.
- ❑ If you're running a contest, use Random.org to choose the winner.
- ❑ Have fun.

BOOKSTORE SIGNINGS

- ❏ Compose a cover letter-style email pitching your book tour. Save it as a draft. You will use it (Copy/Paste) frequently.
- ❏ Research Barnes & Nobles, and other book stores, along your proposed route.
- ❏ Email the CRM requesting a signing on a specific date, remember, weekends are always more successful; but if you're doing weekend events like conventions, you might have to do your book signings during the week.
- ❏ Remember, some CRMs schedule months in advance. All schedule at least 6 weeks in advance, so query early.
- ❏ Upon confirmation, send the CRM an author photo, book cover image, book blurb, and author bio.
- ❏ As you get date confirmations, set up a page on your blog called "Tour" or "Events" or "Sightings," and list all confirmed events. You can utilize a site called BookTour.com, then create a widget to have many places. Automation.
- ❏ Follow up as the dates get closer, ensure the CRMs have what they need. Diplomatically ask if they will have posters in the window and books on the table at least a week in advance.
- ❏ Ensure you are listed on their in-store calendar as well as on the BN.com website.
- ❏ Days of signing: dress up. Be confident. Thank the CRM, hopefully they will be there. Enjoy your free mocha, and interact assertively (not aggressively) with customers.

The following schedules are for normal days, not for marketing pushes. Gearing up for a release, a blog tour, or some other marketing push, your schedule will be nothing but marketing for those weeks. Get back to writing as soon as the push is over, though. You must keep writing regardless.

SAMPLE DAILY SCHEDULE (WITHOUT DAY JOB)

This schedule is for Monday - Saturday

- 6:30am - exercise, at least 3x a week. Walk the dog. Something.
- 7am - check email, read blogs & comment
- 8am - schedule daily tweets in TweetDeck (or chosen program), incorporate links to your most recent blog post; RT and @Reply interesting Tweets
- 8:30am - Update Facebook status and comment on others'
- 9am - Tweet that you're going in for a #1k1Hr #amwriting stint. Then Write for at least an hour.
- 10am - Tweet #1k1hr #amwriting update, quickly respond to any @replies, RT interesting Tweets. Check on hashtags you follow.
- 10:15am - Another #1k1hr. Repeat until noon.
- Break for lunch, briefly. I always eat while I work. During lunch, check Facebook, Twitter, email, etc.
- 12:30pm - Tweet #1k1hr, and write until 2pm.
- 2pm - Finally change out of your PJs. Shower (optional).
- 2:15pm - 5pm. Read. Preferably in the genre in which you write, but read every day. Reading outside your genre and your comfort zone also helps. These things will make you a better writer.
- 5pm - Evening. Change back into PJs. Dinner. Watch *Buffy* and/ or *Doctor Who* with your family. :)

- Sunday Mornings from 8am until noon, write three blog posts & schedule them for the next week. Take 1/2 day off, or work/ write/network more.

SAMPLE DAILY SCHEDULE (WITH DAY JOB)

This schedule is for Monday - Friday:

- 6:30am - exercise, at least 3x a week. Walk the dog. Something.
- 7am - Check email, schedule daily tweets in TweetDeck (or chosen program), incorporate links to your most recent blog post; RT and @Reply interesting Tweets. Let the program run throughout the day while you're at work.
- 8am-noon - Day Job. Use your Smart Phone to periodically Tweet and update Facebook, as those sites are likely blocked at work. Corporate meetings: perfect time to write.
- Lunch break: Read or Write.
- 1pm-5pm - Day Job. Use your Smart Phone to periodically Tweet and update Facebook. If you get done with your daily load early: write.
- 5pm-6pm - Tweet that you're going in for a #1k1Hr #amwriting stint. Then write for at least an hour.
- 6pm - Dinner while you Tweet #1k1hr #amwriting updates, quickly respond to any @replies, RT interesting Tweets. Check on hashtags you follow.
- 6:30pm - Another #1k1hr. Repeat until you're too exhausted to continue. Write at least one hour a day, however. No matter what.
- 9pm - Read until you fall asleep.

- Saturdays: Write 8am until noon. Networking & Tweeting #1k#hr during breaks, etc. Do nothing for the second half of the day. You need some time off.
- Sunday Mornings from 8am until noon, write 3 blogs & schedule them for the next week. Take 1/2 day off, or work/write/network more.
- If you have kids, just give them a box of ice cream bars and sit them in front of the TV. Kidding. No, seriously.
- Family responsibilities, soccer games and ballet classes, etc., will make this even more challenging. Incorporate it into your marketing and tweeting. The important thing is to do what you can and make it a priority. Write something every day.

WORKS CITED

As URLs can become quite long and cumbersome, the information and reference will be below, but most links will be on the "Resource" page of my blog at http://christinerose.wordpress.com.

AUTHOR & PUBLISHING BLOGS TO FOLLOW

- O. M. Grey (http://omgrey.wordpress.com)
- Christine Rose (http://christinerose.wordpress.com)
- Ethan Rose (http://ethanrose.wordpress.com)
- A. L. Davroe (http://aldavroe.blogspot.com/)
- J. A. Konrath (http://jakonrath.blogspot.com/)
- Chuck Wendig (http://terribleminds.com)
- Write It Forward (http://writeitforward.wordpress.com/)
- Jody Hedlund (http://jodyhedlund.blogspot.com)
- Dean Wesley Smith (http://www.deanwesleysmith.com)
- Digital Book World (http://www.digitalbookworld.com)
- All Indie Publishing (http://allindiepublishing.com/)
- Self-Published Author's Lounge (http://selfpubauthors.word-press.com/)

REFERENCED WORKS & SITES
INTRODUCTION

- Anderson, Chris. "Why publishers should focus on the misses instead of the hits." *Publishers Weekly.* 17 Jul 2006. Web. 07 Apr. 2011.
- Bowker. "Publishing Market Shows Steady Title Growth in 2011 Fueled Largely by Self-Publishing Sector." Bowker. 5 June 2012. Web. 21 March 2013.
- Bowker. "Self-Publishing Sees Triple-Digit Growth in Just Five Years, Says Bowker." Bowker. 24 October 2012. Web. 21 March 2013.
- Deahl, Rachel. "BookExpo America 2010: The Changing DIY Ethos." *Publishers Weekly.* 24 May 2010. Web. 07 Apr. 2011.

NEW YORK BIG BOYS & INDEPENDENT PUBLISHING

- "B&N, S&S Term Dispute Continues." *Publishers Weekly*. 25 March 2013. Web. 30 March 2013.
- Agent Query (http://www.agentquery.com/) Free, one-stop writer's resource on the web about literary agents and publishing.
- Bransford, Nathan. (http://blog.nathanbransford.com/) There is a plethora of publishing and querying advice on this blog useful to the emerging author, especially his "Be An Agent for a Day series from April 2009: http://blog.nathanbransford.com/2009/04/be-agent-for-day-here-we-go.html.
- Hedlund, Jody. "Is the Query System Dying?" *Jody Hedlund: Author & Speaker (blog)*. 10 Jan. 2011. Web. 07 Apr. 2011.
- Gardner, Rachelle. "New Query Policy...and 2010 Stats." *Rants and Ramblings: On Life as a Literary Agent*. 8 Jan. 2011. Web. 30 Mar. 2011.
- Predators & Editors (http://pred-ed.com/)
- Query Shark (http://queryshark.blogspot.com/) Read the entire blog. Seriously. Take copious notes. I know there's a lot to read. I know it's a lot of work. This is the price of finding a NY Big Boy.
- Query Tracker (http://querytracker.net)

"SELF-PUBLISHING"

- Bowker (http://www.bowker.com/)
- Carins, Michael. "The ISBN Is Dead." Personanondata. 04 Aug. 2009. Web. 02 Apr. 2011.
- Curtis, Richard. "Behind Publishing's Wednesday of the Long Knives." eReads. 04 Dec. 2008. Web. 07 Apr. 2011.
- Doctorow, Cory. "DIY Publishing: getting Amazon & LuLu to co-exist." BoingBoing. 04 Apr. 2011. Web. 04 Apr. 2011.
- Friedlander, Joel. "Amazon and Lightning Source: The End of an Era?" The Book Designer. 9 Sept. 2011. Web. 18 Feb. 2013.
- Konrath, J. A. "Ebooks and Self-Publishing - A Dialog Between Authors Barry Eisler and Joe Konrath." A Newbie's Guide to Publishing. 19 Mar. 2011. Web. 03 Apr. 2011.

- Lightning Source (LSI) (https://www.lightningsource.com/)
- Smith, Dean Wesley. "Paying for Self-Publishing Help." The Writings and Opinions of Dean Wesley Smith. 25 Mar. 2011. Web. 03 Apr. 2011.
- Strauss, Victoria. "Print-On-Demand and Electronic Self-Publishing." Science Fiction & Fantasy Writers of America. 7 Mar 2001. Web. 03 Apr. 2011.
- Striphas, Ted. "Is the ISBN Still Necessary?" The Late Age of Print. 14 Aug. 2009. Web. 02 Apr. 2011.
- Sullivan, Robin. "CreateSpace Vs Lightning Source." Write to Publish. 14 July 2011. Web. 18 Feb. 2013.

Recommended freelance editors and artists (links on blog)
- Adrienne Crezo, editor.
- TS Tate, editor.
- Helen Ginger, editor.
- Catherine Somerlot, artist. *Avalon Revisited* cover artist.
- Ia Esternä, artist. *Rowan of the Wood* and *Witch on the Water* cover artist.
- James Koenig, artist. *Fire of the Fey* cover illustration.
- J. R. Fleming, artist. *Caught in the Cogs* and *Power of the Zephyr* cover artist.

MARKETING
- Adriani, Lynn. "Web Seminar Debates How Self-Publishing Will Lose Its Stigma." Publishers Weekly. 23 February 2011. Web.
- BittenByBooks (http://bittenbybooks.com)
- Blog Tour Archive links on my blog[1] "Resources" page
- "Facebook Reaches Majority of Web Users." eMarketer. 24 February 2011. Web.
- Howard, Cortnee. "How Publishers Weekly is Ripping Off Self-Pubbed Writers (Open Letter)." The Best Damn Creative Writing Blog. 25 Jan. 2011. Web. 02 Apr. 2011.

---

1 http://christinerose.wordpress.com

- Kaufman, Leslie. "A Novelist and His Brother Sell Out Carnegie Hall." *New York Times.* 16 Jan 2013. Web. 21 March 2013.
- "National Survey Finds Majority of Journalists Now Depend on Social Media for Story Research" George Washington University. 21 Jan 2010. Web. 07 Apr. 2011.
- "Why Most Facebook Marketing Doesn't Work." ReadWriteWeb. 17 February 2011. Web.

Twitter Resources
- TweetAdder (http://tweetadder.com/)
- TweetDeck (http://www.tweetdeck.com)
- Search Twitter (http://search.twitter.com/)
- SocialOomph (http://www.socialoomph.com/)
- FutureTweet (http://futuretweets.com)
- TwitterFall (http://twitterfall.com/) - very Zen
- TwitterFeed (http://twitterfeed.com)
- Tweepi (http://tweepi.com)
- Twiends (http://twiends.com)

EBOOKS & AMAZON
Further Reading:
- Baig, Edward C. "Volume of Kindle book sales stuns Amazon's Jeff Bozos." USA Today. 29 July 2010. Web. 03 Apr. 2011.
- Bosman, Julie. "A Successful Self-Publishing Author Decides to Try the Traditional Route." The New York Times. 24 Mar. 2011. Web. 5 Apr. 2011.
- Bosman, Julie. "Noted Self-Publisher May Be Close to a Book Deal." The New York Times. 21 Mar. 2011. Web. 04 Apr. 2011.
- Campbell, Lisa. "Amazon has '80% online share,' claims new survey." *The Bookseller.com.* 03 Mar. 2011. Web. 12 Apr. 2011.
- Considine, Austin. "eBooks Make Readers Less Isolated." The New York Times. August 20, 2010. Web. Excerpt: "With the price of e-readers coming down, sales of the flyweight devices are rising. Last month, Amazon reported that so far this year, Kindle

sales had tripled over last year's. When Amazon cut Kindle's price in June to $189 from $259, over the next month Amazon sold 180 e-books for every 100 hardcovers…"

- Fowler, Geoffrey A. and Marie C. Baca. "The ABCs of eReading" The Wall Street Journal. August 25, 2010. Web. Excerpt: "A study of 1,200 e-reader owners by Marketing and Research Resources Inc. found that 40% said they now read more than they did with print books. Of those surveyed, 58% said they read about the same as before while 2% said they read less than before. And 55% of the respondents in the May study…"
- Grossman, Lev and Andrea Sachs. "Is Amazon Taking Over the Book Business?" Time Magazine. June 22, 2009. Web.
- Henkel, Guido. "Take pride in your eBook formatting." Guido Henkel (blog). 7 Dec. 2010. Web. 04 Apr. 2011.
- Katz, Kristina. "What I Learned At BEA 2009 Regarding the Future of Writing." Get Known Before the Book Deal. June 4, 2009. Web.
- Miller, Carrie Cain. "E-books Top Hardcovers at Amazon." New York Times. 19 Jul 2010. Web. 07 Apr. 2011.
- Nordin, Ruth Ann. "More on Pricing and Explaining How Smashwords Works." Self-Published Author's Lounge. 6 Feb. 2011. Web. 03 Apr. 2011.
- OpenRightsGroup. "Gaiman on Copyright Piracy and the Web." YouTube. 03 Feb. 2011. Web. 03 Apr. 2011.
- Owen, Laura Hazard. "Five digital lessons from BookExpo America 2012." paidContent. 8 June 2012. Web. 18 Feb. 2013.
- Spector, Mike and Jeffrey A. Trachtenberg. "Chapter 11 for Borders, New Chapter for Books." The Wall Street Journal. February 12, 2011. Web.

Find additional relevant blogs posts and articles of interest linked from the "Resources" page at http://christinerose.wordpress.com.

MARKET TRENDS

- Several resources linked from my blog at http://christinerose.wordpress.com

Summary from 2010 BEA Survey:

Retailers preferred:

- 23% Independent Bookstores
- 22% Major Retailers like Barnes & Noble
- 21% Online Retailers (down from 23% in 2009)

How buyers choose a book:

- 52% Author Reputation
- 49% Personal Recommendation
- 45% Price
- 37% Book Reviews
- 22% Cover Art/Blurbs
- 14% Advertising

REFERENCED & RECOMMENDED BOOKS

- *All A Twitter* by Tee Morris.
- *Dan Poynter's Self-Publishing Manual: How to Write, Print and Sell Your Own Book* by Dan Poynter.
- *Killing the Sacred Cows of Publishing* by Dean Wesley Smith. WIP. Blog Series.
- *Podcasting for Dummies* by Tee Morris, Chuck Tomais, and Evo Terra.
- *Sams Teach Yourself Twitter* in 10 Minutes by Tee Morris.
- *We Are Not Alone: The Writer's Guide to Social Media* by Kristen Lamb.
- *YouTube: An Insider's Guide to Climbing the Charts* by Alan Lastufka and Michael W. Dean.

OTHER TITLES FROM BLUE MOOSE PRESS

Rowan of the Wood
Winner of the 2009 Indie Excellence Award
978-0-9819949-2-5 $12.95 trade paperback
After a millennium of imprisonment in his magic wand, an ancient wizard possesses the young boy who released him. When danger is nigh, he emerges from the frightened child to set things right. Both he and the boy try to grasp what has happened to them only to discover a deeper problem. Somehow the wizard's bride from the ancient past has survived and become something evil.
http://www.rowanofthewood.com

Witch on the Water
Rowan of the Wood: Book Two
978-0-9819949-2-5 $12.95 trade paperback
Cullen thought he had enough trouble surviving school, dealing with his miserable home life, and being possessed by Rowan, a 1400-year-old wizard. But when Rowan's wife, the sadistic vampire Fiana, comes back seeking revenge, Cullen and his band of misfits must do what they can to stop her. This time Cullen's favorite teacher is Fiana's first target.

Fire of the Fey
Rowan of the Wood: Book Three
978-0-9819949-6-3 $12,95 trade paperback
Adventures continue for Cullen Knight and his band of misfits in this third installment of the Rowan of the Wood fantasy series. Still possessed by the wizard Rowan, Cullen settles into his new home with his fire elemental sister, Aidan, and their fey uncle, Moody Marlin. But all is not well. A series of fires raging through the redwoods puts Aidan in the hot seat, as the group looks to her for an explanation.

Power of the Zephyr
Rowan of the Wood: Book Four
978-1-936960-94-1 $12.95 trade paperback
Power of the Zephyr continues the Rowan of the Wood fantasy series with further adventure and magical mayhem. The Freak Squad, as Trudy takes to calling them, confront Fiana in the desert of Northern Nevada. She has developed a cult of mesmerized zombies in an intricate plot to capture Rowan and his wand for herself, once and for all.

Titles by O. M. Grey, Christine's Steampunk Alter Ego:

Avalon Revisited
978-0-9819949-5-6 $12.95 trade paperback
Arthur Tudor has made his existence as a vampire bearable for over three hundred years by immersing himself in blood and debauchery. Aboard an airship gala, he meets Avalon, an aspiring vampire slayer who sparks fire into Arthur's shriveled heart. Together they try to solve the mystery of several horrendous murders on the dark streets of London. Cultures clash and pressures rise in this sexy Steampunk Romance.
http://omgrey.wordpress.com

The Zombies of Mesmer
978-1-936960-92-7 $12.95 trade paperback
Gothic YA paranormal romance novel
Follow Nicole Knickerbocker Hawthorn (Nickie Nick) as she discovers her destiny as The Protector, a powerful vampire hunter. Ashe, a dark and mysterious stranger, helps Nickie and her friends solve the mystery behind several bizarre disappearances. Suitable for teens, enjoyed by adults.

Caught in the Cogs: An Eclectic Collection
978-1-936960-90-3 $12.95 trade paperback
In the midst of war, a beautiful young officer finds love aboard an airship...A woman steals away to fulfill her desire with a phantom lover...A group of thieves seek out a town of women to satisfy their lustful urges, but these ladies have an agenda of their own...

PLUS nine more short stories, angsty love poetry, and twenty-six relationship essays considering topics such as alternative lifestyles, deepening intimacy, opening communication, abusive relationships, and how to end a relationship with respect.

MORE BLUE MOOSE PRESS AUTHORS

Prelude to a Change of Mind
Hidden Lands of Nod: Book One
978-0-9827426-0-0 $9.95 trade paperback
Meg Christmas is found sick unto death in a remote mountain camp. Beings out of legend arrive to save her, emerging from an alternate realm where they live in exile. A quiet, intimate adventure, *Prelude to a Change of Mind* boasts dire peril and brave feats, but also lots of tea with Ekaterina Rigidstick, poems by Jack Plenty, and talks with both about the nature of reality and conditions of being.

Entranscing
Hidden Lands of Nod: Book Two
978-0-9827426-2-4 $9.95 trade paperback
The second book in *The Hidden Lands of Nod* revisits Meg and her friends from the exile realms of the Dvarsh—the metamathemage, Ekaterina Rigidstick, and her cousin, the part-human poet, Jackanapes Plenty—in a vastly different reality twenty years on. This fast-moving follow-on to *Prelude to a Change of Mind* picks up and enlarges the tale of Meg, the Dvarsh, the Thrm, and their collective struggle to save both love and the planet.
http://www.robertstikmanz.com

Fiends: Volume One
978-1-936960-00-2 $35.00 Limited Edition Hardback
978-1-936960-01-9 $12.95 trade paperback
Including Canvas, Tattoo, and Closet Treats, Fiends: Vol 1 is a collection of horror stories by Paul E. Cooley. As a special treat, the author gives his reader a glimpse into the FiendMaster's Scrapbook.

All Blue Moose Press titles are also available in Kindle and other eReader versions. For more information on our current titles, as well as other exciting titles on the horizon, visit **http://thebluemoosepress.com**

GET AUTHOR SIGNED BOOKS DIRECT FROM
THE PUBLISHER and SUPPORT INDIE AUTHORS!

THANK YOU SO MUCH FOR READING.

I HOPE YOU FOUND THIS PUBLISHING &
MARKETING GUIDE HELPFUL.

IF SO, PLEASE CONSIDER WRITING
A REVIEW ON AMAZON.COM AND
GOODREADS. JUST A FEW SENTENCES IS
SO VERY APPRECIATED.

PLEASE SHARE IT ON YOUR NETWORKS
(USING YOUR AMAZON ASSOCIATES LINK,
OF COURSE).

RECOMMEND IT TO YOUR
WRITERLY FRIENDS!

PEACE.

ABOUT THE AUTHOR

Award-winning author of the *Rowan of the Wood* YA fantasy series. Helps emerging authors feel successful by educating them about the publishing industry and marketing their book.

In 2009, Christine was named one of the top 100 Twitter authors by Mashable.com. She spends far too much time tweeting and updating her Facebook status. Many fans have suggested that she should rent space from Starbucks, since she is there so very often.

Christine also writes under the pen name Olivia (O. M.) Grey, author of Amazon Gothic Romance best seller *Avalon Revisited, The Zombies of Mesmer,* and *Caught in the Cogs: An Eclectic Collection.* Ms. Grey has had several short stories and poetry published in a variety of magazines, eZines, and anthologies. Her forthcoming novel *Avalon Revamped* is a horrific look into the darker side of love and sexuality, set in 1880 Steampunk London.

Louise Fury of the L. Perkins Agency represents Christine and her husband (and coauthor for the *Rowan of the Wood* fantasy series) Ethan Rose, as well as Ms. Grey.

Christine needs copious amounts of dark chocolate, frothy mochas, and loving attention.

www.ingramcontent.com/pod-product-compliance
Lightning Source LLC
Chambersburg PA
CBHW060841280326
41934CB00007B/879